SUCCESSFUL INNOVATION

OUTCOMES IN LAW

A Practical Guide for Law Firms,
Law Departments and Other
Legal Organizations

DENNIS KENNEDY

Successful Innovation Outcomes in Law
Copyright © 2019 by Dennis Kennedy

Because of the dynamic nature of the Internet, any web addresses or links contained in this book may have changed since publication and may no longer be valid. The views expressed in this work are solely those of the author and do not necessarily reflect the views of the publisher, and the publisher hereby disclaims any responsibility for them.

ISBN 978-1-7340763-0-1

www.denniskennedy.com

TABLE OF CONTENT

ABOUT THE AUTHOR

D ENNIS KENNEDY (www.denniskennedy.com) is President
of Dennis Kennedy Advisory Services LLC, an information
technology and innovation lawyer, and author well-known
for promoting the use of technology in the practice of law. He
focuses on innovation, legal technology, speaking, writing, and
coaching and is an adjunct professor in the LegalRnD program at
Michigan State University College of Law and also at the University
of Michigan Law School.

Dennis retired as Senior Counsel for the Digital Payments &
Labs group at Mastercard, where he focused on information technology law, fintech law and innovation. His new company will concentrate on innovation, legal technology and productization, including "Legal Innovation as a Service" packages and the Kennedy Idea
Propulsion Laboratory.

Dennis is a Fellow of the College of Law Practice Management
and former chair of the board of the American Bar Association's Legal Technology Resource Center. Dennis wrote the legal technology
column for the ABA Journal for many years and has co-authored

several books, including *The Lawyer's Guide to Collaboration Tools and Technologies* (2nd edition, 2018) with Tom Mighell and *Making LinkedIn® Work for You* (2019), with Allison Shields. He co-hosts The Kennedy-Mighell Report podcast on the Legal Talk Network, and has written his blog, DennisKennedy.Blog, since 2003.

Dennis was one of the first lawyers with a website (1995). He can be found on Twitter at @denniskennedy and on LinkedIn at www.linkedin.com/in/dennismkennedy.

INTRODUCTION

A s in the case for many books, I wrote this book because I looked for a book like this one and could not find one. So, I decided to create one. You know that you are, at heart, a writer when that is the path you take to solve that problem.

I've recently realized that innovation is a visible thread that runs through my career, especially in the major transitions and changes I've made. That insight took me quite a while to see for myself, although others have pointed it out to me.

Especially in the last year years, I've been part of many conversations about change, innovation, and new approaches in law. Many of the same questions keep arising. This book tries to provide answers to many of those common questions, but, more importantly, it points you in ways to answer those questions for yourself.

This book offers a distilled version what I have learned and experience over the years. It also grew out of several recent articles of mine that appeared in modified forms in some of the longest chapters in this book. I expect to continue to learn and update this book with new editions from time to time, perhaps even annually. It also lists many resources I've found useful and makes them available in one place. I wish I'd had that when I started this journey.

There are four target audiences in the legal industry I had in mind when I wrote this book:

- ► Innovation team leaders (whether with the title of chief innovation officer or not)

- ► Business leaders wanting to drive innovation (managing partners, general counsel, CFOs, COOs, CIOs, chief strategy officers, business development leaders, and the like)

- ► Individual innovators, including those who aspire to moving into one of the first two categories
- ► Clients and customers of legal service providers who want to see their providers bring them more innovation

Others will find this book useful as well.

The vision and mission of this book is simply to help forward-looking innovators in the legal world get needed guidance and a framework for increasing their chances of innovation success and decreasing their chances of innovation disasters.

Here are some answers to questions you might have.

Is this a blueprint, template, step-by-step playbook or one-size-fits-all masterplan?

No. It is a practical guide, focused on successful innovation outcomes. Great innovation programs are each successful in their own ways. The formats and steps they use can be quite different. Even if you follow every step someone else does, your results will differ, probably in not so good ways. Consider how many sports teams try to copy the approaches of championship teams and never even come close. I wanted to map out the major things you need to consider and provide some insights, tips, and questions for you.

Are there other approaches you might consider?

I specifically called this "a practical guide" and not "the guide" for a reason. It captures and offers my unique knowledge, experience, and insights gained over time. It's opinionated and, at times, swims against the current. Kind of like me. I try to point you to resources that I've found helpful, including those that challenge my opinions and have changed my approaches. I'd love it if this book motivated you to write a book of your own.

Are you against process improvement?

Not at all. In this book, I, from time to time, argue that we focus too much on process improvement and incremental innovation in the legal world. I like to question that approach and in Chapter 14, I playfully challenge the people, process, then technology dogma, with the purpose of getting you to think that through rather than simply accept it. My perspective is that process improvement has an important place, as long as that's what your goal and vision are. However, if you give me the choice, I'd rather be playing in other areas of innovation.

Why don't you include templates and checklists?

If you work through some of the exercises and tools in this book, I think you will also conclude that the better business model for me would be to sell templates and checklists as a separate book. Seriously, though, I wanted to write this book and I was not convinced that there was a demand for templates and checklists. Let me know if you think otherwise and, if I see sufficient demand, I'll consider adding them to a second edition.

Why didn't you cover X, Y, or Z in this book?

I knew there are likely to be future editions and that I couldn't cover everything. In any project, you have to make a choice about when the project is done and what gets left on the cutting room floor. Or the project tells you itself that it is done. There were elements of both happening with this book when I made the decision to call it done. Also, I tried to point out in this book in many places at what points it might make sense to get additional help.

What in writing this book surprised you the most?

Two things. The first is how much I've come to rely on visual tools, especially the value proposition canvas. The second is that advisory boards were not in my original book plan, but they now seem one of the most important elements of a successful innovation plan. Perhaps that comes from my own recent experiences on advisory boards, but the logic is so compelling to me.

How is this book organized?

This book is divided into eight sections.

1. **An Innovation Primer**, in which I cover innovation definitions, whether legal innovation is different from any other innovation, optimization vs. innovation, the adjacent possible, innovation models, and the ten types of innovation.

2. **Core Principles**, in which I cover why-what-how, the importance of customer focus, business models, diversity, quantity vs. quality, constraints, people-process-technology, lawyers and ideas, and external ideas.

3. **Creating and Improving Your Program**, in which I cover game plans, a basic roadmap, requests to make, personnel, teams, internal selling, small wins, road shows and demos, innovation committees, bringing in help, coaching and mentoring, and advisory boards,.

4. **A Taxonomy of Innovation Tools**, in which I cover the scientific method, experimentation, brainstorming, prototypes, MVPs, visual tools, feedback loops, metrics, process improvement, advanced techniques, and other innovation tools.

5. **Examples of Innovation Efforts**, in which I cover three innovation efforts that will work, selling to GCs and other decision-makers, panel convergence, key client programs, collaborating with other legal organizations, and my TechPrompts(TM) example.

6. **Risk and Portfolio Management**, in which I cover evaluations and audits, risk alignment and portfolio management, increasing and decreasing investment, and changing course and pivoting.

7. **Handling a Few Hard Things**, in which I cover dealing with failure, unexpectedly hard stuff, barriers and breaking through them, and self-care.

8. **Action Steps, Tips, and Resources,** in which I end with some simple action steps you can do immediately after you read them, collect 57 tips for you, and point to some useful resources you can use to learn more. I also tell you a bit more about me and what I'm doing.

However, I don't want to be the introducer who takes too much time away from the presenter and presentation. Let's get started.

PART I

AN INNOVATION PRIMER

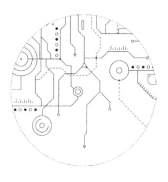

1

Defining Innovation

"Innovation is applied creativity."
—Alan Weiss

"Innovation" is a four-syllable word that is easy for us to say. It's so much harder for us to do than to say. "Definition" is a four-syllable word that, especially in the legal industry, brings innovation efforts to a standstill. If you have ever been in a seemingly-endless meeting with lawyers wanting to have "consensus" on a "definition "of "innovation," you will recall a growing sense of despair that any work will ever get done or that the meeting will ever end.

Yet, here we are, at the beginning, and it does make sense to find some common ground on what we mean by "innovation." Or, at least, what I mean and what I'm hoping to gently convince you that you should mean.

Going back to the origins is always helpful.

The entry for "innovation" at https://www.etymonline.com/word/innovation tells us that the use of the word arose in the 1540s. It is a "noun of action" (I like that term), from the Late Latin innovationem, a past-participle stem of innovare, meaning to change or renew. Digging deeper, we find "in," which generally means "into" in Latin and "novus," meaning new. We might interpret that as bring something new into being. The word also commonly gets defined as "renewal" or "restoration." The etymonline.com definition of "a novel change, experimental variation, new thing introduced in an established arrangement," becomes quite useful, because it associates innovation with the interplay of new and old and introduces the important notion of experimentation.

To the extent we might actually find consensus on a definition, we turn to the modern index of consensus, Wikipedia. To be frank, Wikipedia is a bit vague and disappointing: "Innovation in its modern meaning is 'a new idea, creative thoughts, new imaginations in form of device or method.'"[sic] It goes on to refer to "the application of better solutions that meet new requirements, unarticulated needs, or existing market needs" and "the provision of more-effective products, processes, services, technologies, or business models." Business models, to me, are an essential part of innovation. I have difficulty calling something an innovation if it does not involve a rethinking of the existing business model.

Two other minor, but interesting, points from the Wikipedia entry. First, there is a reference to the antonym of innovation, which is "exnovation." Exnovation means an explicit philosophy and practice of not innovating. More specifically, it occurs "when products and processes that have been tested and confirmed to be best-in-class are standardized to ensure that they are not innovated further." That makes me think of "planned obsolescence" or even hubris. It might be a good word to throw casually into an innovation meeting for fun.

The second point is that, in the early days of the word, "innovation" had a negative or pejorative connotation. People used it as a "synonym for rebellion, revolt and heresy." That gives it a bit of an edge.

A few other definitions I like that will help get you thinking:

1. "Innovation is change that creates a new dimension of performance."—*Peter Drucker*

2. "Innovation is the specific instrument of entrepreneurship... the act that endows resources with a new capacity to create wealth."—*Peter Drucker*

3. "The process of creating a product or service solution that delivers significant new customer value."—*Anthony Ulwick*

4. "Innovation is the embodiment, combination, and/or synthesis of knowledge in novel, relevant, valued new products, processes, or services."—*Dorothy Leonard and Swap Walter*

5. "[A] great idea put into practical use, shared, scaled and sustained to transform the ways we live and work."—*Womenininnovation.com*

6. "An innovation is a feasible relevant offering such as a product, service, process or experience with a viable business model that is perceived as new and is adopted by customers."—*Gijs Van Wulfen*

7. "The implementation of creative ideas in order to generate value, usually through increased revenues, reduced costs or both."—*Jeffrey Baumgarner*

8. "[U]sing something new, or something known, but in a different way, a different time or a different place."—*Lady Barbara Judge*

9. "Turning an idea into a solution that adds value from a customer's perspective."—*Nick Skillicorn*

10. "Innovation is significant positive change. It's a result. It's an outcome. It's something you work towards achieving on a project. If you are successful at solving important problems, peers you respect will call your work innovative and you an innovator. Let them choose the word."—*Scott Berkun*

11. "An invention or intervention—that shows evidence of a valued solution, garners support of decision makers,

and offers mutual benefits for a wider community—by drawing insights from diverse people across several related fields."—*Ellen Weber*

12. "Innovation that can offer solutions to existing problems where conventional approaches have failed to deliver results holds the key to a more inclusive development model—a model that can enhance access, affordability, service delivery and improve the lives of the people at the bottom of the economic pyramid."—*Sam Pitroda*

If you are caught in a meeting where attendees are trying to reach a consensus definition of "innovation," remember that even the experts can't agree on that. The key takeaway for me from this chapter is that innovation is a "noun of action" and "innovate" is a verb. Get to work and let others talk. Making something new that creates customer value takes work.

While it is important to get alignment on your approach to innovation, it's OK get quickly get to close enough on the definition. The quote from Alan Weiss at the beginning of this chapter is a pretty good starting point, especially when you consider it in the context of creating new value for your customer.

 PRO TIP: Get to work on innovation, however you define it, and let others talk.

2

Is Legal Innovation Different?

—————————

I f you think that the discussions around a consensus definition of innovation can be mind-numbing, try getting a group of lawyers in a room debating what "legal innovation" might mean or if it can even exist. Or whether "legal innovation" is different from "plain ol' innovation."

Short answer: no.

Let's start with the fundamental point: every minute you are debating these issues, you are not innovating.

For some people, the term "legal innovation" brings up the notion of "legal exceptionalism." Many lawyers have the belief that every single thing that they do is unique and cannot be duplicated because it can only be done by lawyers.

As I'll illustrate in a minute, I don't like to narrow the scope of innovation.

On the other hand, I'll admit that the term "legal innovation" can occasionally be helpful. It can reduce the amount of early opposition to an innovation effort or program in a legal organization by making it seem that legal innovation is something that the legal world needs to do and, in fact, actually does.

I also like to use "legal innovation" from time to time because it opens up the possibility of at least three different types of innovation efforts in law. You might be able to add more.

1. **Innovating the day-to-day practice of law as it impacts legal professionals.** Think of the lawyers, legal professionals, and the firm as internal customers.

2. **Innovating the delivery of legal services to clients and third parties.** Think of clients and third parties as external customers for whom the innovation should bring new value.

3. **Innovating the legal system itself.** Think of the general public, court systems, or governmental systems as the customers, rather than your clients. Access to justice efforts fall in this category.

When I taught my first class called "Delivering Legal Services" in the LegalRnD program Michigan State University College of Law, we used design thinking techniques to create a new kind of "legal service." I let the students be as creative as they wanted to be. One of my favorite results was from a student who looked at how to create an expungement clinic for people with minor misdemeanors who could not afford a lawyer. Michigan had just passed the legalization of marijuana and expungement was (and still is) an important issue.

The student's approach was to focus on one key aspect of the clinic, and I guarantee the idea will surprise you. The student defined the problem to be solved as getting clinic customers to the clinic, especially in the Upper Peninsula of Michigan where the clinic was going to be piloted. The solution: a free ride-sharing and reservation program like Uber or Lyft to get customers to the clinic to their appointments and get them home again. Even better, the service would provide an incentive for riders to fill out more extensive surveys than other clinic participants might be willing to do. That data could be used as feedback to improve the clinic and its services, and provide insights for similar pilots elsewhere.

This concept was innovation by any standard and any definition. If we limited the scope of what could be "innovation" to something purely "legal," we would have missed this idea and the benefits it could bring.

Call it what you must, but don't use the definition as a limiter or a blocker to getting to the work to be done.

 PRO TIP: Legal innovation simply means applying innovation techniques in the legal world, in a variety of different dimensions.

3

Optimization vs. Innovation

————————

W hen I've taught law students about design thinking and facilitated design thinking sessions, I've been struck by how often I'm the outlier. I love generating ideas until we get all of them out of our heads. Only then do I like to organize, shape and move on to the implementation process.

In my experience, that puts me in a group of about ten percent of people in the room: the idea people. Most lawyers fall into a different group. I call them the process or process-oriented people. Staying too long in the realm of idea generation makes them uncomfortable. They want to move right away to the "how" and say things like "we have to define the process and get it right first" or "we have to focus on quality ideas."

There is obviously a place for both types. It's good to recognize them both.

A key area of difference reveals itself in the willingness to start with a blank canvas and not be wedded to existing processes. Process people are likely to think of innovation as improving an existing process rather than replacing an existing process. Idea people like to replace things or try something new.

You can often identify process people by the way they turn to words like "optimization" and "improvement" when they define and consider innovation.

I want to touch on the important distinction between innovation and optimization. I don't want to be didactic, but it's important to keep in mind. I think of optimization as a subset of the broader world of innovation. Some refer to optimization as "sustaining innovation" or "incremental innovation," as we'll learn later in this book. However, some actually separate optimization from innovation.

I focus on two differences. First, when you concentrate on optimization of processes, you tend to overlook possible changes to your business model. In fact, your business model is unlikely to change. You are, by definition and by temperament, looking to improve what you already do. Second, you tend to lose sight of the customer and notion of customer value. You are so focused on finding efficiencies and improving processes that your efforts can get divorced from customer needs and customer value.

An easy check on what you are doing is simply schedule time to ask "why?" you are adding features, creating efficiencies, choosing your roadmap, and why it would matter to customers.

What you want to avoid is doing the wrong thing and what no one wants, and then trying to get better and better at that. 'Nuff said.

 PRO TIP: While focusing only on optimization can have great value, it also narrows your perspective and causes you to miss bigger innovation prizes.

4

The Adjacent Possible: Learning and Borrowing from Other Professions

---

Lawyers have an annoying tendency to think that everything that they do is unique, that it's all custom, and that only lawyers can do it. As I mentioned, I tend to call this attitude "legal exceptionalism." Others, maybe even you, use even less flattering terms.

As a result, lawyers are often reluctant to use the classic and proven innovation technique of getting ideas from other sources outside of the legal industry.

Innovation rarely means something completely new. In most cases, it's taking existing ideas and approaches and recombining them in new ways.

Steven Johnson has used the term "adjacent possible" to mean "a kind of shadow future, hovering on the edges of the present state of things, a map of all the ways in which the present can reinvent itself." This is a useful concept and, in practical terms, encourages us to consider a wider range of possibilities and to look outside our own silo for inspiration, ideas, and examples that have worked elsewhere.

We have a toolbox of innovation approaches to start from: subscription models, gym membership models, marketplace platforms, client portals, mobile apps, and much more.

In his highly-recommended book, *Creative Strategy: A Guide for Innovation*, William Duggan sets out a while innovation process based on picking and choosing among standard approaches that have worked in other contexts. It's a highly useful and effective way to work on innovation and I revisit it in Chapter 40.

Similarly, Larry Keeley's essential book, *The Ten Types of Innovation*, sets out a framework of the ten primary innovation business models discussed in more detail in Chapter 7. It's difficult for me to think about creating an innovation project without running it through this grid.

Three examples for you to consider.

1. **Doctor-Patient Portals**. One of my favorite developments of the last few years has been the adoption of standard patient portals by my medical providers. I can schedule and reschedule appointments, pay my bills, check test results and other records, get referrals to specialists, and do simple things there rather than wait on hold for someone to answer a call. It's made my experience with the medical world so much better than before.

   In my law school class, I used this as an example and talked about the reluctance of law firms to adopt this model. I've talked to many people who've told me that they hate to call their lawyer to get a copy of a document because they are required to talk to the lawyer and inevitably get a 0.5 hour charge for the call. In almost all of my students' projects, an online client portal was a key part of their business plan.

2. **ClariLegal**. ClariLegal (*Disclosure: I'm on ClariLegal's advisory board.*) is an online marketplace platform that provides a way for customers to create a simple RFP for litigation support projects, make the projects available for bid by vetted vendors, and then compare the bids in a structured and straightforward way to make fast decisions and find the best vendor for the project. At its core, it is a market-maker platform targeted to certain projects, with several other innovation

models incorporated. Markets, of course, have been around since humans first lived in groups. Here, Clari-Legal takes that model and moves it into the legal field. There are other examples of market platforms in the legal world. Keep your eyes open for them.

3. **FoundationLab**. FoundationLab (*Disclosure: I'm on FoundationLab's advisory board.*) is a legal product design company. As I'll discuss later, moving swiftly from idea to prototype is an essential part of the innovation process. FoundationLab (https://www.foundationlab.co) looked at this potential roadblock and used the subscription model as the core innovation building block. The result is an annual subscription that allows a customer to submit ideas and get quick prototypes on a monthly basis for a fixed fee. One somewhat unexpected value for a customer is that, in a year, a chief innovation officer could show a dozen concrete prototypes in flight as evidence of the work they've done.

Subscription models have created a lot of interest in the legal world, especially in small firm practices and as an alternative to billable hours. My own offering of Legal Innovation as a Service grew directly out of looking at subscription models in a productized service context, even though it evolved in different direction.

 PRO TIP: Look outside the legal silo and learn the standard types of innovation and business models. Think more in terms of recombining ideas from other sources than creating completely new ideas out of thin air.

5

Innovation Models

———————

There is no "one truth path" to innovation. However, there are some standard models. You don't need to invent the models and you can (and should) try to work within the standard models, especially when you start.

In this chapter, I will discuss the generally-accepted "four categories of innovation" standard approach. I like the way it is succinctly explained in Greg Satell's article, "The 4 Types of Innovation and the Problems They Solve." (https://hbr.org/2017/06/the-4-types-of-innovation-and-the-problems-they-solve) The article also has a great quadrant chart that illustrates the relationships among the models.

The four models approach focuses on the problem to be solved. Satell focuses on two questions: "How well can we define the problem?" and "How well can we define the skill domain(s) needed to solve it?"

Here are the four models, as described by Satell:

1. **Basic research**: where neither the problem nor the skills domain is well-defined.

2. **Disruptive innovation**: where the problem is not well-defined, but the skills domain is

3. **Sustaining innovation**: where both the problem and the skills domain are well-defined

4. **Breakthrough innovation**: where the problem is well-defined, but the skills domain is not.

Satell gives examples and recommends approaches within each model.

Others make some variations to this four-model approach. I like an approach that looks at the quadrant in terms of better vs. worse performance, and higher cost vs. lower cost.

There are several other approaches to categories of innovation. Some of them might appeal more to you than others do. For example, the term "incremental innovation" seems to have become more popular in recent years. You will want to become conversant in the language of innovation models that the people you interact with use.

A word about disruptive innovation. Disruption and disruptive innovation have very precise meanings. In the legal industry, the term "disruptive" has been thrown around so much that it's difficult to know what anyone means by it.

I've found that it's best to avoid using "disruption" or "disruptive," or at least to use it only when you are talking about its precise meaning, which comes from work done by Clayton Christensen. The idea is that a disruptive product or service comes in at the *very low end of the market*. The incumbent players decide that the new product or service is not competition or a competitor, giving the new product or service time to establish itself and evolve. By the time the incumbents realize the competitive risk, it may well be too late for them to respond.

If you pressed me to make a prediction, I'd say that disruptive innovation in legal technology and/or legal services is likely to arise out of something originally created for the access to justice market that evolves to the point that it makes the leap over to legal services at large. One key indicator would be that legal incumbents describe it as "not a competitor." Keep your eyes open when you see that phrase used.

 PRO TIP: Understand the foundation innovation models (and their variants) and become fluent in the language of these models.

6

Ten Types of Innovation

———————

'm often asked whether there is one book that people should read to get started on their innovation journey, especially in the legal realm. In large part, that's why I wrote this book. I didn't have one to recommend for helping people get successful innovation outcomes in law.

However, the book I always recommend is *Ten Types of Innovation*, by Larry Keeley, Ryan Pikkel, Brian Quinn, and Helen Waters. It is a detailed playbook, with many examples of actual efforts that have succeeded in all types of industries.

At the book's core, however, is, as the title suggests, a model that describes innovation as falling into ten different types. The authors developed this taxonomy in 1988 and have continued to improve it. It's an extraordinarily useful model. I recommend reading and re-reading the model and the examples as you start, continue, and seek to improve your innovation efforts.

This quote succinctly describes the author's approach and is something that all innovators should contemplate: "***Innovating requires identifying the problems that matter and moving through them systematically to deliver elegant solutions***."

We sometimes underestimate the importance of achieving *elegant* solutions. The authors list the following ten categories:

1. **Profit Model**: making money

2. **Network**: connecting with others to create value

3. **Structuring**: organizing talent and assets

4. **Process:** using unique or superior methods

5. **Product Performance**: developing distinct features

6. **Product System**: creating complementary products and services

7. **Service**: supporting your offerings

8. **Channel:** delivering your offerings

9. **Brand**: creating unique branding

10. **Customer engagement:** fostering compelling interactions

Models 1 through 4 are further categorized as "configuration" models, in which the focus is on the inner workings of the enterprise and its business system.

Models 5 and 6 are "offerings" models, in which the focus is on your core product or service, or a specific collection of products and/or services.

Models 7 thorough 10 are "experience" models, in which the focus is on customer-facing elements of the enterprise and its business system.

Innovation can happen in one or more categories or types. In fact, the most powerful innovations happen when you mix types or use multiple types in combinations. When you start to do that, you see how useful the ten types of innovation approach can be.

In addition to book's insights, practical playbook approach, and helpful examples, I like the emphasis on innovation as both a discipline and work that requires discipline, the way it keeps you focused on business models, and how it helps you experiment with mix-and-match methods of finding innovations.

As I mentioned, this book is the one that I recommend most often, so that's what I want to do here.

 PRO TIP: Keep the book Ten Types of Innovation at the core of your innovation library and, better yet, give it a place of honor on your desk so it's always at hand.

PART II

CORE PRINCIPLES

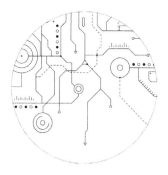

7

Why–What–How

———

A useful concept is innovation is that there is a process of moving from WHY to WHAT to HOW. This is a sequence.

What you want to do in this sequence is to extend the time you spend on WHY and WHAT and hold off on moving to HOW as long as you can.

The WHY stage is understanding the customer's problem or job to be done. Some even advocate a "5 Whys" approach to get to the real issue or problem. At the heart of this approach is LISTENING to the customer.

With the understanding and clarity, you can move forward to WHAT might be done. You're still resisting moving to the HOW.

Only then do you move to HOW. Is it a technology approach? A process approach? A people approach? A productization approach? A new business model? A combination?

It should not surprise you that the better you understand the WHY, the easier the HOW becomes.

 PRO TIP: Linger in the WHY stage as long as you can.

8

Focus on the Customer

B ecause I include "increasing customer value" in my definition of innovation, it should be no surprise that I put the customer, internal or external, at the center of the innovation process.

Lawyers often disagree with me on that focus.

The objections typically come in three forms.

1. **Clients Don't Know What They Need (Unless I Tell Them).** Lawyers often believe that clients don't know or can't understand what their legal needs are and, therefore, don't really add much of anything to the legal innovation process. The lawyers believe that only they can determine what the clients need and then provide it. Not surprisingly, what lawyers determine that clients need looks a lot like what the lawyers are already doing or offering in the way of services.

2. **Steve Jobs Didn't Ask Customers What They Wanted.** I love it when this argument is made by a lawyer using a 5-year-old laptop running Windows 7. Whether or not this is a myth about Steve Jobs (and his team), the argument is actually a variation on #1, that the lawyer knows more than the client does about what the client wants.

3. **Customers Would Have Asked for a Better Horse, Not a Car.** Again, we can recognize this argument as a variation on "the client doesn't know or understand." It's also interesting as a version of the usefulness of constraints. If you can't make the horse better, what do you do? Are we focused so much on the horse that we don't realize that the problem is actually one of transportation from Point A to Point B?

If we return to the WHY → WHAT → HOW discussion, you should be able to see that the customer uniquely knows the WHY part and can offer excellent input on the WHAT, but might not be as concerned about the HOW (other than it doesn't make their work and business more difficult or expensive than before).

The three objections I mentioned fall primarily in the HOW stage. That's the problem.

Your customers (internal or external) will also be about to tell you what the pain point is or the job to be done, especially if you facilitate that discussion. They will know the pains they need to alleviate and the gains they hope to achieve. That's the information and insights that a customer-focused approach brings. And it shows that you are concerned about and listening to them.

If you can nail the WHY phase with your customer, the rest of the process will be easier and your odds of success will increase. Most important, you have an engaged customer ready and willing to participate in an experiment.

PRO TIP: You have to get the customer into the conversation at the beginning. Find ways (some discussed later) to facilitate those conversations in directed and productive ways.

9

Business Models

I n my personal view of innovation, and that of many others, taking a hard look at business models and changing business models are core elements of what innovation is. If you don't examine business models, you are likely to stay in the realm of process optimization. That's not necessarily a bad thing, if that is your goal, but, many times, it is not.

The notion of business models can be a difficult one for many lawyers, as they are rarely taught the topic in law school. The business models they are most likely to know are the billable hours model and the pyramid partner-associate model.

I'll use the term "business model" to mean the design of a business to capture a commercial opportunity. Business models are part of the overall business strategy. They describe how the enterprise creates, delivers, and realizes value on an ongoing basis. Business models can change and be improved over time. Some use the term "business model innovation" to cover the process of creating, improving, or changing business models.

There are many types of business models. The extensive list at https://www.scrum-institute.org/blog/A-Comprehensive-List-of-Business-Models-To-Accelerate-You-and-Your-Business is a good starting point. Just reading the names of some of these models, and others you can find elsewhere, will give you some new ideas.

In legal, there is a push from customers for movement from billable hours models to flat fee, value, and subscription models.

You will also get my attention if you talk about platforms, ecosystems, or "eliminate the middleman" business models.

A good understanding of business models will help you align your innovation offering to a good business model for the offering and what you want to accomplish. You might also establish pilot projects using several different business models. Often, the blockage that you find on innovation projects can be cleared by changing the business model you consider. Even the simple process of looking at your idea in a grid of different business models can provide huge insights and new ideas.

PRO TIP: While you will probably gravitate to several favorites, it's a great idea to learn (and maybe even memorize) a lot of the standard business models to give you a framework and context for your efforts and to help you communicate in the language of business.

10

Diversity is Essential

There are times, usually when I'm in a room full of white men who look and think in the same ways, that the idea I'll discuss in this chapter is the most controversial opinion I can state in the innovation setting. However, it's my core belief.

Diversity, in and of itself, is not only a good thing in innovation efforts, it's essential to success. Really, it is.

And I don't mean paying lip service to diversity by saying we all might look the same and come from similar backgrounds or all have legal educations, but we have "diversity of perspectives." Ask someone outside that narrow band of perspectives how diverse that band is. It's almost always a narrow slice.

I spent many years at Mastercard, by any definition a global company. I was in conversations and meetings with people from all over the world. I always gained fresh insights from new perspectives and approaches other than my own. It always surprised my how quickly the assumptions you made about how a successful product in one country would be just as successful in another country would be brought into question when you included people from the second country. It's great to get a challenging dose of reality.

I've lately been recommending Caroline Criado Perez's book, *Invisible Women: Data Bias in a World Designed for Men*, which among many other things, points out the actual physical dangers of not including women in design and scientific research, all based on actual data.

The risk of taking a non-diverse approach is groupthink. Group-think has given a long history of bad results, including ill-conceived wars. Looking to avoid it by design is a great way to move innovation efforts toward success.

No need to just take my opinion. There are many studies that support the proposition that simply diversify your team by gender, race, nationality, and other factors leads to better results.

I now like a team where the mix of people makes me feel just a little bit at unease because it creates more energy, forces me to listen and learn, and helps me feel what it's like to be different. All of these things stimulate creativity and innovation.

Are you checking on a regular basis how diverse your formal and informal teams are? Is someone missing from the table who could give you real-world feedback on your assumptions? Are you hearing all the voices that need to be heard?

 PRO TIP: Take a look around the room at your next meeting. And the one after that. And the one after that.

11

Quantity vs. Quality

Without doing an exhaustive study, I'm still comfortable stating that every core resource on innovation emphasizes the importance of generating a large quantity of ideas at the beginning of innovation efforts. There are many reasons for this, not the least of which is that the last ideas that arise often are the ones that generate the breakthroughs.

If you have lots of ideas, you can notice patterns, start to combine ideas, and create connections between completely different ideas (what might be the connection between "food trucks" and "free expungement clinic? There are a lot of them). If you are using the technique of putting post-it notes with ideas on the wall (which I recommend), people can see results, momentum, and progress.

Having a lot of ideas also helps create a mindset of experimenting and prototyping. Participants see that there are many things to try and many ideas that might work. This mindset is important because most of your first innovation efforts, like startup businesses, are likely to fail and must be adjusted as you try them, get customer feedback, and test assumptions.

I have been in brainstorming sessions with legal professionals where the issue of quality over quantity came up within just a few minutes. The air came out of the balloon of creative flow immediately. You want to get the ideas out and then sort and evaluate later. I cannot emphasize this point too much or too often.

The biggest problem I have with focusing on quality of ideas at the beginning is that we don't know what quality is until after we see how things play out with customers and the market. To me, "quality" often means alignment with existing business model or the way things are done. This approach creates problems in times of change or when current legal services delivery model is under pressure.

Two examples for you to consider.

I facilitated a "rethink" design thinking session a while back, with 30 to 40 participants, all of whom were lawyers and legal professionals. I wanted to issue the challenge of having 1,000 post-it notes with ideas on the wall by the end of the brainstorming portion of the session. I also allowed people to prepare in advance and bring a list of ideas. The other organizers thought that my 1,000-idea challenge was too over the top, and we decided not to give a target number (although I might have let the number 500 slip in my introductory remarks at the session). If you took out the notes posted by the facilitators in advance of the session to seed ideas, we ended up with about 150 post-it notes on the wall.

Since a good portion of the notes were comments, non-specific, and aspirational rather than actionable, the number of big new ideas that were generated was small. It was still enough to end up with eight solid action items, but they were more in the nature of incremental improvements and priority clarifications than "rethink" proposals. Not a bad result, but less than hoped for by me.

My other example comes from my Delivering Legal Services class at Michigan State University. I gave the students the general problem of creating a misdemeanor expungement clinic in a rural area. In a short time, they had generated a few hundred post-its, from the perspectives of customers, student interns, and the courts, with ideas for data-gathering and feedback. Some of the ideas were exciting and original and some were offered to a pilot expungement clinic project in the summer of 2019. There were also other ideas that could be experimented with elsewhere or tried later.

Is there a magic number of ideas to generate? No. Fewer ideas at the start will result in fewer options going forward and more initial investment in those options and reluctance to change them. There's a lot of psychological research that bears this out.

The more ideas the better. The "crazier" ideas the better. The fewer constraints on what ideas are allowed the better. Get the ideas out. The sorting, organizing, and selecting comes later. I often say that I'm simultaneously the best and the "worst" person at a controlled brainstorming session, because I take the quantity notion to heart. I definitely generate a lot of ideas. That's the fun part.

 PRO TIP: Always emphasize from the beginning that idea generation is about "quantity," but reassure participants that they will get to focus on "quality" later.

12

Constraints and Beautiful Constraints

─────────────

'm always intrigued when a discussion of creating a new innovation plan or project turns immediately to how much money is needed and what the budget request should be.

My most successful innovation projects almost always began with a budget of either zero or the cost of one software license. Funding came as a result of a successful results. In fact, I'm known for once presenting the results of a non-funded innovation effort and explicitly not asking for any funding, only to be told that a significant budget would indeed be found for the next phase, even if I said I didn't need it. That impressed people. However, having funding, in my opinion, hurt the momentum of the project because people took their eyes off the ball and thought about budgets rather than experiments and results.

The fact is that innovation often is associated with constraints. Look at the example of M-Pesa, the payment system in Africa. Because the banking, technology and other infrastructure was not in place and there was no money to build it, M-Pesa grew a payment system originally based on trading prepaid cellphone minutes that now has staggering levels of adoption in many African countries. Others were focused on finding budget for traditional Internet cables and other infrastructure.

There's a book called *A Beautiful Constraint: How To Transform Your Limitations Into Advantages, and Why It's Everyone's Business*, by Adam Morgan and Mark Barden, that sets out the case for the importance of constraints (and overcoming them) in innovation efforts. If you can't do X, what can you do instead? That's when you get creative.

Whitney Johnson, in her book, *Disrupt Yourself*, which I consider essential for innovators, also focuses part of her process on looking at constraints and using them in positive ways.

In design thinking exercises, there is a standard approach that I like where you first ask participants what they would do to solve a problem if they had a small amount of money. Let's say $2,000. After they work for a while under that constraint, you then ask them how they would solve the same problem if they had a very large budget. Let's say $20,000,000. The idea is to remove the financial constraint and get you to think bigger. I like to introduce a new constraint in the large budget example and require you to spend the whole amount. Another variation on this is to do a 2X vs. X/2 budget or even a 10X vs. X/10 budget exercise.

By the way, if you ever participate in an exercise like this, the "cheat code" for the small budget exercise is to think of ways to use part of the small budget to raise more money.

You want to turn constraints from stoppers to temporary blockers that can either be overcome or help show you a different, often better, path. There are always many ways to reach the same goal.

I've learned over the years that if I'm complaining about something, it generally means that the problem is not important enough to me to do more than complain. If the problem is important enough, I do something about it. Your attitude toward constraints should be similar. Is it a barrier or a wall or is it a challenge and opportunity? Attitude counts for a lot.

 PRO TIP: Make a list of the constraints that you believe that you face. Simply writing them down will change your attitude. Then decide whether they are barriers that stop you and why. The others are opportunities to help you move in new directions.

13

People, Process, and Technology

The phrase I've heard most often over the years about legal innovation is "People, then process, then technology, in that order." I have no doubt you have heard this many times. In many circles, it's considered revealed and accepted wisdom.

I wouldn't consider myself an innovator if I didn't take a close look at this assumption and challenge it. That's what I'll do in this chapter. Spoiler alert: my feeling is that this approach leads you to optimization rather than innovation, and to incremental or sustainable innovation rather than breakthrough or disruptive innovation. I'm not saying that's a bad thing at all. It's just important to make sure it matches your vision and mission.

I struggle with the "people, process, then technology" formulation in general, but especially when a priority order is placed on them. Each of these components is changing and dynamic. There is an interplay, a cause-and-effect relationship, and an ecosystem that this linear statement understates. And it suggests that each effort has a certain sameness in approach. I'm not convinced.

The statement also comes from a different framework than my own innovation framework. Where does increasing customer value fit in? Aren't business models missing from the equation? Where is the problem to be solved and what about the customer's job to be done? Does this order mean that I can't experiment with changing the order?

Let's look at the elements. I want to give you some insight into my approach.

People

Oddly, even though this element of the priority makes sense, it quickly gets very confusing. What people? If it's customers, that makes sense to me. What about the team or decision-makers? There are other categories of people as well. Do we mean the whole ecosystem of people? Are we really talking about culture more so than individuals?

People can be really difficult. They resist and obstruct change. They think they want one thing and they really want something else. They change their minds. They leave. They can be difficult to work with in so many ways. Sometimes, you need to plan for people like potential customers who you don't know much about.

Process

I had a number of jobs over the last 45 years. I worked with many very bad processes and made them work, often with work-arounds, hacks, and adjustments. It's rare that you see a process, especially in law, that seems to work well. People just adapt.

As I've mentioned, when you focus on process, you tend to move toward optimization and incremental innovation. These might give you good results, if that's what you want. For me, focusing on process also feels backward-looking and keeps you within the existing framework. I'm never sure how business model change fits into a process focus. However, process innovation can definitely result in measurable improvement to customer value. The question is whether there were bigger questions you needed to ask. Good process people ask those questions, but once you are immersed in a process, it's difficult to break out of the process optimization mindset.

Technology

There are several adages about technology that say, in essence, "innovation is not technology" or "innovation is not about technology." Fair enough. We all want to avoid a solution, especially a technology solution, that is searching for a problem to solve and at which we throw lots of money.

I always want to be sure that people who advocate a "technology last" approach either are not afraid or technology or unaware of what now exists. Perhaps the key development of our time is that cloud services like Amazon Web Services allow us to create prototypes and deliverable products with a surprising number of features in a day or so and very cheaply. Sometimes people underestimate what you can easily do with technology or do not fully understand what technology already exists and what it can do.

I like to challenge the approach where you wait until the end on technology. I have done successful innovation projects that arose out of simply wanting to see what a new technology could do. In other words, once I became aware of the technology, the ideas flowed from thinking about the technology first. In some cases, knowing what technology you already have can drive ideas and directions.

The other objection I have to making technology your last priority comes from the number of times I've heard people tell me about a great idea they are working on that literally is already available in other products in the market. I've long felt that the biggest hurdle for most legal organizations is not knowing what legal technology already exists.

In a way, I'm having a little fun with the standard "people, process, tech" maxim, but I also have some serious doubts about accepting it uncritically. To me, it's a good example of how, as an innovator, you want to flip assumptions, question accepted wisdom, and experiment with different approaches to see what you learn.

 PRO TIP: What happens if you look at a project and invert the maxim of "people, process, then technology" and frame your effort as technology, process, then people? Does it provide a new insight or framework?

14

Lawyers and Ideas: A Limiting Factor?

A general rule in innovation, especially in brainstorming, is that in any group of people, there will be plenty of ideas. In fact, in the average group of ordinary people, generating a lot of ideas will never be a problem.

That rule, unfortunately, does not seem to apply to groups of lawyers.

Lawyers tend to be an inhibiting factor in brainstorming. They are quick to see problems, reluctant to participate, eager to impose restraints, like to dominate discussions, and are unwilling to offer spontaneous ideas. Lawyers will also overfocus on definitions and rules for the idea event, if they participate at all. The negative body language of a room of lawyers asked to "ideate" can be something to behold and psychologists could write volumes on the subject.

It would be too simplistic to say that lawyers cannot justify ideating in the framework of the "billable hours" model, but, if you talk to lawyers, you will find that is an issue.

A lawyer's training in "issue spotting," problem analysis, and risk reduction also contributes to the difficulty lawyers have with idea-generation, especially when combined with the often-observed lawyer trait of always needing to be right and never to look bad or wrong. And, perhaps worst of all, the cult of busyness ("I'm so busy that I have to cancel your meeting to show everyone how busy and important I am") makes even the simple of act of getting lawyers into the room on time, and for the whole session, extremely difficult.

You can generate your own long list of other factors. Simply put, the average lawyer is not good at all in generating large numbers of new and untested ideas. There are obviously some exceptions, but this general state of affairs, especially because lawyers are usually the decision-makers, makes early stage ideation involving lawyers a difficult hurdle.

However, you need not despair. There are several techniques that you can use to optimize lawyer engagement in ideation.

1. **Seek Their Recommendations of Who Should Participate.** Allow the lawyers that you want to participate to recommend their own proxy if they cannot attend. This approach will help you identify someone who might be willing and able to participate and who is respected by the recommending lawyer. The recommended lawyer will also feel an obligation to participate because they were recommended. Flattery gets you somewhere.

2. **Use Lawyers as a Way to Get Client Involvement.** I find that ideas generated by a group of lawyers tend to end up being, well, rather lawyerly. The key to innovation is increasing customer value. Rather than engaging reluctant lawyers in the ideation phase, solicit their involvement in finding clients who would participate.

3. **Bring in External Idea People.** There are many people, especially those in the field of legal technology, strategists, adjunct professors, and law students who can generate uninhibited ideas. Imagine if you had me contributing new ideas to your session rather than the grumpy partner who is staring at his smartphone with a scowl the whole session, except for interrupting to say that an idea is bad or won't work or otherwise to rain on your parade.

4. **Study Brainstorming and Facilitation Strategies and Tactics.** There is some science around ideation, especially group ideation. What you are seeing is not unique. People have found ways to address problems and achieve good results. Dig into the research and articles.

5. **Move Lawyers to a Later Point in the Process.** Lawyers excel at sorting, organizing, and evaluating ideas. Consider pushing back significant lawyer involvement until that part of the innovation process.

 PRO TIP: You must deal aggressively with the "lawyer inhibition factor." A creative idea might be to get a group of lawyers to "brainstorm" a process that optimizes their ideal roles.

15

External Ideas

An under-appreciated aspect of idea-generation is the negative results that can arise from the "echo chamber" effect. If you use the same people, all from the same organization, over and over, you will limit the number of ideas you get and fail quickly into the realm of "we tried that before and it didn't work."

I discuss the important of diversity in Chapter 11, but in this chapter I wanted to touch upon the approach of bringing in external ideas and perspectives.

In many cases, the all-important voice and perspective of the customer is missing from the initial idea-generation session. To the extent customers are involved, they are allowed only to react to ideas that have been already fleshed out and finalized. Customers are pitched to or lobbied instead of invited into the ideation process. There's a big difference between the two approaches.

Adding customers is, conceptually, the easiest first step. Some organizations are reluctant to do this for fear they might hear something they don't like from customers or similar reasons. You will want to address and overcome those concerns.

Another good source of external ideas is people who are not familiar with your services, processes, or approaches, especially if these people might become potential customers or referrers.

There is another source I'd like you consider. There are external experts, authors, and "thought leaders" who have unique experience, subject matter and industry expertise, insights, and perspectives. Simply tapping into that knowledge base, bringing one or two of these people into your sessions, might well supercharge your idea-generation process. In my experience, many of these people enjoy getting the chance to do this. Consider it.

 PRO TIP. Not all of the best ideas are contained within your organization. Look outside in thoughtful and strategic ways.

PART III

CREATING AND IMPROVING INNOVATION PROGRAMS

16

Basic Plan / Roadmap and Budget

———————

W hile I'm a firm believer in the adage that no plan survives first contact with reality, usually in the form of a potential customer, I equally believe that having a plan is essential, even if only for the exercise of organizing your thoughts that goes into creating a plan.

Revisiting the original plan in three years is likely to take you on a trip down memory lane to a place that is far different from where you ended up and following a much different path that your plan set out. That's not a bad thing.

However, it illustrates that, while planning and getting a written plan in place is important, you do not want to overextend or over-complicate the planning process or the planning documents.

I like to reduce the planning, either initial or annual, to only three components: a business plan, a roadmap, and a budget. In an ideal world, none of these should be more than one page. Each is designed to both frame the necessary conversations with decision-makers and capture the meeting of the minds and agreements about the innovation effort.

Business Plan

I love the business planning approach embodied in the one-page "business model canvas" I discuss in more detail in Chapter 35. It captures the key elements you need to think through and your answers to core questions. There is a similar model called the "Lean Canvas," which might appeal to some of you.

I suggest simply capturing the information in your canvas and writing it in an easy-to-read (bullet-pointed) narrative form. Keep it to one page and think of what the key questions that your target audience will want to have answered. I'd put the answers in bold. You might even consider adding a Frequently Asked Questions or FAQ as a schedule or appendix to the plan.

There are hundreds of books and other resources on how to write a business plan. Don't overthink this. Grab a copy of Jim Horan's *The One Page Business Plan for the Creative Entrepreneur* and follow the steps in it. If a decision-maker really wants detailed business plan before you begin, make them ask you to create one, but still keep it short. The standard Small Business Administration business plan template will do the trick in most cases.

Road Map

The modern human loves visuals, maps, and infographics. A simple visual road map of what you expect to accomplish, and the phases for doing so, will take you a long way. There are plenty of examples on the Internet. Find one like and you will be well on your way.

Budget

I'm one of those people who likes to ask decision-makers what their budget is or what amount they have in mind before I offer a number of my own. More often than would expect, the number in their mind is higher than the number in your mind.

If you have a range to work with, you can sketch out a budget that fits in that range, preferably at or near the top it. But don't stop there.

For me, a budget actually means three separate budgets, ideally shown in three columns for easy comparison. The first is what you think it will take to accomplish what you have in mind. The second is what you really would like to have. The third is a gasp-inducing "here's what we could do if we jumped in feet first" budget.

No surprise here: you want to move the decision-maker off of #1, closer to #2, and let them have the chance to think about #3. Psychologically, it's difficult not to move to the middle option.

Two important points. First, lawyers, as a group, hate math, so keep the numbers simple. Second, any reduction in proposed budget must clearly result in a deliverable in the plan being removed. Do not get caught in a "do more with less" game. Your message should be that you did your homework, and the numbers are solid.

Three sheets of paper, all designed to move the ball forward and get decisions and agreements. It does not take weeks for a decision-maker to read three pages. It can take weeks for them to get through 50 or 100-page documents.

These documents will frame the conversation, push toward a meeting of the minds, and, in final, revised form, memorialize the agreements for the innovation effort.

 PRO TIP: Keep your written plan or roadmap simple, keep it short, and keep the reader's attention.

17

Game Plan for Getting Started

———

So, you've been put in charge of your organization's innovation efforts. Or maybe you are a team of one for yourself. Or maybe you are taking over an existing effort. How do you get started?

The good news is that there are many possible game plans. The bad news is that there are many possible game plans. I've written this book as a guide to help you be the hero of your own innovation story. You'll need to make the decision about what works best for you. And you must be prepared to adjust on the fly as you get more data.

If it were me, I'd start with a significant (perhaps all-day) facilitated (perhaps by you, if you feel comfortable doing it) design thinking event that included a diverse group of customers, stakeholders and members of your team, and a few people who are regarded as forward-thinking. Avoid including only people inside your organization, if you can. Getting an interested client or two would be a big plus.

One other vital thing. In the corporate world, we usually had someone known as the "executive sponsor" for big new projects and initiatives, someone in senior leadership who had advisory responsibility for the effort, could lobby for the group with management, and who had some skin in the game. I will not sugar coat this; if that person does not exist or is not present and active at the beginning, think of your time on the projects as merely a career a portfolio builder and start updating your resume because you will be leaving sooner rather than later.

I also think that, if your plan is to focus on certain types of techniques (e.g., design sprints), then your plan for getting started should darn well come out of a design sprint like the one you intend to offer. You can call it "eating your own dog food," as they say, somewhat unappetizingly, in the tech world, but, if you don't trust your own service offering, why should anyone else? If you use the technique and people see the results, you'll have advocates.

Your approach to starting an innovation will reflect what category of innovation program you want to build. I see four types, but you might see more.

1. **Mission or Vision Programs.** Here the focus is on WHY. You develop and get agreement on a specific vision or mission statement that is short and memorable. You the use that statement to test everything that you plan to do. You don't need (or want) specific details from the beginning. For example, the vision statement for my Legal Innovation as a Service offering is "Helping forward-thinking legal organizations improve innovation efforts." Any offering I want to create must fit this mission.

2. **Focused, but General, Service or Product Offerings.** Here the focus is on WHAT. The innovation program looks to provide a primary service or product offering (e.g., 4-day design sprints, productization of legal services, or an innovation lab). Your efforts will be to keep improving how you deliver those offerings and use the results, while concentrating only on customers who would benefit from the tools.

3. **Predetermined Products or Improvements.** Here the focus is on HOW. You might have already determined that you will provide customers with a contract lifecycle management tool, an e-discovery repository tool, or similar offering, and your efforts will be to keep improving those products.

4. **"Check the Box" or "We Have to Do Something Now" Programs.** Let's be honest, many of these types of efforts exist. "Just get me something so I can say we do innovation." A term you hear to describe these efforts is "innovation theater." In rare cases, these efforts can turn into something positive, but the focus is not on the customer, but on perceived internal needs. Your focus will be on showing effort, getting publicity, and producing a good innovation "show." If you are in one of these efforts, always ask for more money, at the beginning.

It's important to determine into which category you fall. I'm not going to make value judgments, although I have a preferred approach. If you align your efforts to the approach you are taking and stay focused, you can get good results. The key, however, is staying focused.

Remember that you can adjust an existing effort to better align with one of these categories too.

Tools like the Value Proposition Canvas and the Business Model Canvas (discussed in Chapter 35) can be valuable in this process.

 PRO TIP: Determine which of the four categories your effort falls into and try to get at least a one-day design thinking or strategic planning event scheduled.

18

Requests to Make if You are Put in Charge

_____

For many years, I worked in large organizations. Because of my legal technology expertise, I got the request from time to time about what I'd estimate it would cost do to upgrade legal technology along the lines that I thought best.

I loved to say, "I'd estimate about $5,000,000." The response would inevitably be "$5,000,000?!!!!" And I'd say, "Well, maybe $6,000,000," as if they had thought my number was too low. The response was usually, "I was thinking a million or two." And I would say, "For the first year? I was only talking about the first year."

A couple of observations. First, I was testing to see how serious they were about doing something and how transformative they really wanted to be. Second, you'll notice that I move the project budget significantly above zero without even asking. Finally, I knew that there was no time like the beginning to ask for everything you want.

In most cases, I scared the asker away, but I needed to know how serious people were and how willing they were to support an effort if they wanted me to be involved or lead it.

So, what should _you_ ask for at the beginning? Although the same things are important in subsequent years, your leverage is greatest at the start.

As an aside, if you are asked to start a program, pause dramatically, sigh, and say, "I'm inclined to say no, but let me think about it and we can talk in a couple of days. I'm flattered that you thought of me to do this." Play a little hard-to-get, even if it is your dream opportunity.

First and foremost, you need to create a list of requests based on what's most important to you. And make all of those requests. Leave nothing on the table. Think the budget issues through carefully. You might simply ask for a budget of $X, while I might ask for how we will address the need to exceed the budget when it arises and what justifies budget increases in midcourse.

Some of the main items on my list, if I were you, would be:

1. **Who will be the executive sponsor?** In a law firm, that person, at a minimum, must be on the firm's management committee, but ideally would be of a "C-Level" (CEO, COO, CFO, CLO) stature.

2. **What category of effort will this be?** Ideally, you will know which of the four categories of programs I discussed in Chapter 18 and ask for the program you are creating to be of that category.

3. **Will I have direct access to clients and how will that happen?** For me, a "no" on this one is a deal-breaker.

4. **How will we set expectations and milestones and how is success determined?**

5. **What will be the approach on the inevitability of failed projects?**

6. **What will the approach to staffing be?** Will I be allowed to invite lawyers to assist without it negatively impacting on their compensation, reviews or careers? In many ways, this question comes down to whether non-permanent participants will get billable hour credit.

7. **What training and assistance will I be able to obtain for myself and team members?**

8. What conferences and other programs will I be able to attend and what trade associations and other groups will I be able to join?

9. Is this considered a Business Development effort, an IT effort, or something else?

10. What management and firm meetings will I be on the agenda for and be able to make presentations or provide updates?

11. How will my compensation, including bonuses, be determined, especially if we create a product that generates a lot of revenue?

That will get you started. You have their attention at the beginning, so don't leave questions unasked.

 PRO TIP: Make your list of questions and get them answered. The fact that you are willing to ask hard, thoughtful questions shows that you are the right person for the role.

19

Personnel and Who's in Charge

The success of your program will depend on your people, including you. Do you have the right people? Do you have enough of the right people? How do you find, hire, onboard, and retain the right people? What do you even mean by the "right people"? And are there innovation personality types that you should be looking for?

In some cases, you might find yourself pressed into service to lead an innovation program with a small group of reluctant volunteers. In some cases, you might inherit the leadership of an existing innovation team. In some cases, you might have a blueprint, a charter, and a budget. And, in some cases, you will be making up the program as you go.

A big part of your effort will be continually sketching out your people needs and charting when you will need to fill those needs. I don't know of any single checklist for what jobs and what skill sets make for an ideal innovation team. The interplay among you, your team, your projects, and your vision will bring you to your people choices. The better defined your vision is, the better people choices you will make.

As a general rule, you will want to start with generalists (people who fill several roles) and fill in specialists as the needs for them become apparent. Demonstrated experience, ideally in the form of a portfolio of projects, is a must. In the early days, customer interaction will be the job of everyone, so err on the side of people with good communication skills and likability.

As I forcefully stated in Chapter 11, building a diverse group is essential in innovation efforts. Whether you start with a version of the Rooney Rule (that you commit to interviewing at least one diverse candidate for every position) or something less formal, don't let yourself drift into hiring a homogenous group or only people who look and think like you do.

There have been some studies on desirable innovation personality traits. Debra Baker at Growth Play (http://www.growthplay.com) has gathered a lot of survey data about innovation traits in the legal market and learned a lot about innovation traits. If you know the success factors, that can help you hire great candidates.

From my perspective, people who will thrive in the innovation setting either self-describe themselves as "creatives" or have a track record of creative work. I like to see people who have a record of writing, artistic pursuits, video, design, music or similar pursuits in their previous work, as hobbies, or even in school work. I want to see a spark, a different way of looking at things, and an instinct for self-expression or communicating in different media. You might want to do some simple surveys and tests to get an idea of the personalities and motivations that you are dealing with.

The trick with creatives is that they work best when freed up to do things in their own ways. For many of them, the best way for you to manage them is to set their path, get out of their way, and clear obstructions for them. It takes special skills to manage creatives. Anything perceived as "micromanagement" is anathema to creatives. Cool projects, great tools, and creative workspaces are bigger motivators than money and traditional benefits, but if a creative ever feels underpaid (which translates to under-appreciated), you will feel the breeze of the door closing as they walk out the door.

There are resources to help you manage these types of people. Positive, constructive, and consistent feedback is vital, but short, informal, regular check-ins can go a long way in keeping them happy.

Involve your team in the selection of new members, including suggesting candidates, interviewing, and selection. Read Susan Cain's book, *Quiet: The Power of Introverts*, to get some insights into the introvert personality and do not assume that everyone likes team activities, especially those outside work hours.

I also believe that it's best for innovation leaders to step away from managing individual projects as quickly as they can and focus on other strategic activities.

Finally, be an advocate for your team. If there is blame, accept responsibility for the team publicly and deal with any team issues privately. If there is a win, make it a team win publicly, but single out top contributors privately with the team and reflect their accomplishments in evaluations and bonuses.

 PRO TIP: Do not hire a group of people who look and think like you do.

20

Teams

---

nnovation thrives on teamwork and is definitely a team sport. However, innovation teams are often built with unique, opinionated, and iconoclastic individuals. It's quite difficult to put together creative teams and keep them together for the long haul.

In this chapter, I want to look at teams in the innovation context and point out an approach to team-building that I find especially useful.

I learned a great exercise for startup businesses that has application when you build teams for innovation programs, in part because innovation programs are a lot like startup ventures.

First, you map out the "C" roles required in a successful, growing business: chief executive officer, chief operating officer, chief financial officer, chief human relations officer, chief marketing officer, and so on. Then, you look around the table and see who is going to take on the functions of each of those roles, because all those functions really do exist.

If you are a solo, you have ALL of those roles. Congratulations! No wonder it seems like you don't have enough time to get to the work you thought you'd be doing. If there are two of you, you need to divide up the functions between you, looking for aptitude, fit, and willingness. And so on. If you see a complete deficit in any of the roles, you will see where you probably need to consider outsourcing the function.

Your goal, over time, is to start transitioning yourself and others out of the roles and functions that are not best fits and into just the role(s) and function(s) that are best matches. A simple concept, but difficult to execute. However, this mapping helps surface the important tasks at hand.

When putting together your innovation team, you'll want to do a similar exercise. If there is a priority for a chief marketing officer and it's not your strength, you're still stuck with doing that role until you find your replacement. That might change your hiring priorities.

In Whitney Johnson's essential book, *Building an A Team*, she talks about S curves in the context of teams. In her book, *Disrupt Yourself*, she looked at S curves in the context of individual development. It's an adaption of an approach to business growth first developed by Clayton Christensen and others.

Here is the S curve concept. When you start something new, you have to learn a lot, you feel overwhelmed, you have to work hard, and you need a lot of help. This is the low end of the S curve, or the beginner curve.

Then, the curve slopes sharply upward, as you've learned the basics and start to get good at what you are doing. You feel knowledgeable, more in control, work feels easier, and you don't need a lot of help. As people sometimes says, "I'm tired, but it's the good kind of tired."

Finally, at the top of the S curve the curve flattens out and starts to slope downward. You start to feel bored, that there's nothing new for you to learn, work seems repetitious, and you start reading articles about burnout (well, you do toward the end of the curve). However, you are also recognized as a subject matter expert, a keeper of the history and knowledge of the group, and a coach and mentor.

In Johnson's approach for individuals, she argues that the key to your career is to be able to jump from the S curve you are on when you get to the top of the curve to your next S curve and start again at the beginner level. You might be able to see this pattern in your own career changes.

In *Building an A Team*, Johnson applies these principles for Individuals to teams, with fascinating insights. First, if you are aware of where your people are at on their S curves (and she has tests to help you determine this), you can manage them in accordance with their place on the S curve. For example, rather than let someone proceed to burnout at the top of the curve, you can help them transition to a new challenge and new S curve. You can also assign projects accordingly or help people have a good mix of projects.

Most interesting, she's collected data that shows the best teams have a mix of 15% at the bottom of the S curve, 70% in the middle (or "sweet spot") of the S curve, and 15% at the top of the S curve. As your team grows, you can start to use this data to create a team that matches this mix. And then manage to it.

A few other observations about teams.

A great culture is essential for great teams. Mike Lombardi's book, *Gridiron Genius*, looks at teams from a sports perspective, but contains a wealth of information about what makes great teams work (this might not be the best book for New England Patriots haters) and the crucial importance of culture. Highly recommended.

Recent research at Google had indicated that one of the most important, if not the most important, factors in team success is psychological safety. Whitney Johnson puts it directly and succinctly: "How do we help our colleagues and direct reports feel safe?"

There are tons of literature and resources on teams. You should have no trouble creating a list of your own. Add team-building courses and seminar to your annual budget request for education.

Building and/or being part of a great team is an amazing experience that you will always look back on fondly. Unfortunately, I've found that you often only realize that you were part of a great team after the experience is over, because you are so focused on the work you are doing and the challenges you are facing. It's so important to build celebration into the completion of big projects. The best team leaders I've known also went the extra step of including the spouses, partners, and even children of team members in that celebration. It makes a big impression and shows consideration that the work has impact on them as well.

PRO TIP: Consider looking closely at where you team members are on their career S curves and building for the 15%-70%-15% mix based on placement on the S curve. (See Whitney Johnson's *Building an A Team* for details.)

21

Internal Selling

———————

I f you lead an innovation effort, one of your biggest jobs will be as an advocate for your program, for your people, for your results, and much more. If what you are good at is innovating, managing, and delivering results, advocacy might not be your biggest strength. It might, in fact, be your biggest hurdle, especially once you realize it means selling, and internal selling at that.

The good news is that internal selling is a skill that can be learned and you can delegate or get help with some, but not all, of it. At some point, you must be the voice of the program.

Let me return for a minute to the notion of having an executive sponsor. The sponsor can open doors, help train you, and provide invaluable feedback. Add these to your list of reasons to have an executive sponsor in place and meet with them regularly.

I usually tell people that they need to be able make their pitches in a very short period of time, perhaps two to three minutes, and then invite questions. I'm no longer sure that lawyers even have a two-minute attention span anymore before they will interrupt or start checking their smartphones.

There are many resources for making pitches and "sales" presentations. Ultimately, you want to find something that feels authentic to you. Oren Klaff's *Pitch Anything*, for example, has some great ideas and techniques, but will only work for you if you feel comfortable with them. If you feel this area is a weakness for you, make sales and pitch skills training part of the request you make when you set up the program.

Lawyers are a difficult and impatient audience. I advocate a simple three-step, even a three sentence, approach, with the next action step that you want embedded in the pitch so the listeners can discover it on their own. Remember, humans love and respond to the "rule of threes."

What do I mean? Here are three examples.

Pitching a solution

1. Customers have told us that the problem they want to solve is X.

2. Customers indicate that they would see these things as a great solution for X

3. Our proposed solution aligns with the customer's goals and desires.

4. Result: The listeners "see" on their own that the proposed effort makes sense.

Pitching a Next Step

1. We have been running a pilot or experiment and have obtained results and data.

2. The results and data show us X.

3. Because we are seeing X, it makes sense to continue, change direction, stop, or continue to run the experiment and get more data.

4. Result: The listeners "see" that the data itself is driving us toward a course of action.

Pitching for Additional Staff or Funding

1. A pilot or experiment has been started with customer.

2. Customer has indicated that it would like to proceed and invest $X.

3. It would take an additional $Y or specific additional staff to satisfy customer desire and commitment.

4. Result: The listeners "see" that customer commitment justifies additional investment.

As I said, there are many approaches you can take, but, remember, lawyers can be a tough audience.

 PRO TIP: Find yourself a guide or "Yoda" to help you learn how best to sell to your internal audience and enlist your internal champions.

22

Small Wins

'll always remember my Dad coaching me in baseball and saying, "just put the bat on the ball; don't try to kill it."

I'll discuss high-risk, high-return long shots in the context of a portfolio approach in Chapter 48. However, always swinging for the fences, to continue, for a moment, the baseball analogy, has never been a good strategy.

Innovation requires experiments and analysis of results. Many experiments will fail. The key is to learn and move on.

When leadership of an organization looks at an innovation program, they want to see results and momentum. If you invest in one giant effort and it doesn't pan out or it takes far longer than you ever imagined, you invite questions and criticism. People start to lose confidence in you.

It is so much better to focus on putting the ball in play or, better, putting more balls in play, and showing a number of wins, even if they seem like small victories to you. Your small win might be huge in someone else's eyes, especially if it helps add a new client or prevent an old client from leaving.

Your goal here is to show a continuing series of small wins to build confidence, show results, and set the stage for permission to do bigger efforts. It's a building process.

What might that look like? Imagine you had a goal to produce one new simple prototype of a productized legal service a month and start testing it. In a year, you would be able to point to twelve prototypes created and in flight. Some might have failed, but others will have worked or provided valuable data. Those small wins also provide valuable data for decision-makers when they consider budget approvals for the following year.

 PRO TIP: Build some small wins into your project roadmap.

23

Road Shows and Demos

A special, and highly effective, form of internal selling is using demos and road shows (especially in multi-location organizations) to "show and tell" what you are doing and plan to do. This approach gets the word out, enlists supports and, perhaps most important, helps you identify potential talent within your organization.

This "show and tell" approach also makes sense to educate customers and show them ways they can benefit from the program.

There's not a lot of mystery to this approach, although it is important to remember to take advantage of the opportunities not just to sell, but to collect data and get feedback. For example, you might believe that a week-long design sprint is what customers want. When you present your design sprint offering to key customers, you might get feedback that, while they like the concept, it's too big of a commitment at this point. However, a "demo day" event might be the right starting point for now. Make the adjustment and work with them to give them what they want.

You will want to determine what your program should be. I'd suggest an introductory presentation to establish context, demos, and plenty of time for Q & A, but you'll need to determine what works best for your audience.

You will also need to pay attention to logistics: budget, staffing, scheduling, and travel. There can be a lot of moving parts and you should expect some rescheduling and postponements.

Three words about live demos: don't do them. Create a great video to show where everything works exactly the way you want it to. Many things can go wrong during a live demo. Why take the chance?

 PRO TIP: A well-conceived "show and tell" road trip can kickstart your program and might even generate more projects than you can handle. That's a good thing.

24

Innovation Committees

I t's often been said that committees are places where ideas and innovation go to die. Working with lawyers is synonymous with committees. Unfortunately, committees are necessary evils. How do you make the best of them?

Mission and Purpose

Get clear on what the purpose and mission of the committee is. In some cases, the committee is really the innovation team itself. In other cases, it might have an oversight or approval role. Or it might be something else entirely. Committees with unclear missions are often disasters.

Name

I prefer to call any committee I'm involved with a "working committee." That sets a clear expectation: if you don't want to work, this committee is not the one for you. The name should align with and reinforce the mission and purpose of the committee. You often see names like "steering" or "advisory" committees. Personally, I'd avoid the term, "oversight committee," but I like to have a light management touch on me. That might be why I like the term, "steering committee." It feels like the committee only has a light touch on the wheel when it's needed.

Agreements

Committees run best when there are clear expectations, responsibilities, and agreements. These run the range from the most basic—attend all meetings, all meetings start exactly at the time scheduled—to tailored and specific—committee members will participate in X number of design thinking events. I like to get agreement on agendas in advance and to get agreement on action steps at the end of meetings.

Run a Good Meeting

The good news is that are tons of resources on running good meetings. We all have different styles. Do some research and find approaches that appeal to you and might work best with your team. It's good to ask for feedback on how meetings are working and how they might be improved. Meetings, dreaded as they can be, are a great place to try experiments.

How Long Committee Meetings Should Be

In volunteer boards I've chaired, I'm probably best known for saying, "A meeting needs to be as long as it needs to be, and no longer." If there is an agreed-upon agenda and people do the prep work, meetings do not have to be long. For a standing committee, I like to shoot for thirty-minute regular meetings rather than sixty minutes or more, unless the agenda requires a longer time. I do not like to cancel standing meetings. People need to adjust their schedules to the meetings and make accommodations if they cannot attend them.

Frequency

Everything flows from mission and purpose. Some committees need to meet more often than others. Some can have quarterly or annual meetings. For a standard innovation committee, I would expect monthly meetings.

Changing the Committee

Especially for advisory or steering committees, it's important to get fresh perspectives. You might have a core group and rotate people on and off every year. You might put people on staggered, multi-year terms. There are a number of options.

If you find that certain topics are taking a lot of agenda time in meetings, consider moving the topics to subcommittees and allocating agenda time at the main meeting to short subcommittee reports.

There is nothing worse than having people on committees who don't want to be on them. Have the necessary conversation, address the issue, and move on to someone new, if that is an option. If the problem person can't be removed, there are techniques for improving their participation. For example, a practice of starting meetings exactly on time and never summarizing what latecomers have missed will help them learn to show up on time.

Remember, often the requirement is simply that there be a committee of any kind at all. You can take advantage of this and create a committee that helps you the most and provides value for committee members.

 PRO TIP: Own your meeting style and set your agendas in advance.

25

Bringing in Help

———

As I like to say, innovation is a team sport. The more of a burden you put on yourself, the more likely you are to burn yourself out. That can happen no matter how creative and enjoyable you think the work is. That's the reason that the last chapter in this book is on self-care.

Especially if you are an idea person, others are likely to think that "innovation" is easy for you. If others flatter you by calling you an "innovator," you'll tend to take responsibility for most of the process. And, in so doing, you risk becoming the "bottleneck" or "roadblock" and bringing progress to a crawl. That's not a place you want to be or a place your team wants you to be.

The fact is that even a rudimentary mapping of the roles and responsibilities in any innovation effort will show that it is not a one-person job and, even with a team, there will be some roles and skill sets that you will not be able to cover.

That's why a simple roles-and-responsibilities mapping exercise is vital.

Some of the needs will be apparent. If your team does not include a "numbers" person, you'll need help, internal or external, with budgeting. If you are clearly a "process" person and not an "idea" person, you'll need help, internal or external, generating ideas. Idea people often need project management help. If you lack subject matter, technical, or industry expertise, you can try to learn on the fly as you simultaneously launch an innovation program, or you can get expert help.

Ideally, you will take a hard look at your need for outside help as part of your budgeting process and build whatever you need (consulting, training, coaching, and the like) into your request.

By the way, asking for approval for spending on outside help is a great, practical way to gauge your organization's commitment to innovation. If you can't get approval to buy everyone on your team a copy of this book, alarm bells should be going off. If there is a $5,000 innovation conference that it makes sense for you to attend, will the organization balk at that or encourage you to send more members of your team? It's a nice little feedback loop.

We all get into trouble when we are unable or unwilling to ask for help. Try to determine what your strengths are and focus on them. Get help where you need it. This is just one of the reasons an executive sponsor, mentor, or coach is so important.

 PRO TIP: It's hard, but you have to be able to ask for help. People often are willing to give you more help than you'd expect. In fact, the help you might ask for might be easier for them to give than what they were afraid you were going to ask them for.

26

Coaching and Mentoring

———

At some point, probably sooner rather than later, you will realize that creating and running an innovation program is a very big job. It will also be one that increasingly pulls you away from what you like best (innovating and creating) and fills your time with activities you didn't expect (meetings, sales efforts, political infighting, sorting mixed priorities, scheduling, hiring, replacing key team members who leave for other opportunities, approving expense reports, even more meetings, and so much more).

In the last chapter, I talked about getting help. In this chapter, I want to focus on two related, but different, forms of help: mentoring and coaching.

Mentoring

Mentoring can mean many things, but to me, mentoring is finding the wise guide (your Yoda) who helps you, listens to your questions, makes subtle suggestions, asks you hard questions, points you gently in the right direction, and always sees the bigger picture that you cannot. Many mentor relationships last a lifetime.

Unfortunately, you can't just run out to the mentor store and buy a mentor off a shelf. Typically, a mentor relationship is something that you recognize rather than go out and find. And, often, it is the mentor who finds you. I love the quote, "When the student is ready, the teacher appears."

In other words, you probably should not request a mentor in the list that you make before you accept the role. However, if you push hard for an executive sponsor, you greatly enhance the chances that that person will become a mentor for you, or introduce you to someone who becomes a mentor. But there is no guarantee.

More than likely, you are likely to find mentors in the larger innovation community, in the people in your organization with whom you do great work, or in the clients you work with. That's why it's so important to participant in innovation organizations, attend conferences, and, yes, participate in social media. One of the great things today is that you might find a mentor anywhere in the world.

Coaching

Coaching should be thought of a limited period of targeted assistance for which you pay for the service. Coaching is different from mentoring, but you might get similar results in some areas.

There are coaches of every kind these days, from life coaches to personal trainers, but I haven't yet seen the rise of innovation coaches. In some cases, coaches have certification organizations or standard approaches and techniques.

Coaches tend to address specific needs or weaknesses. For example, if you are not experienced or comfortable speaking in public, you might get a speaking or presentation coach to help you reach a desired level of competence. This is another instance where it makes sense to build coaching into your budget request.

How do you find the right coach? I've personally had great success with two different coaches. I found each of them in a different way. Nothing about those finding processes is helping me find a new coach. It's largely going to be a case of defining what you want, finding someone who matches that description, and determining whether there is a "fit."

That said, it would be unfair of me to end there. Here are some of my suggestions.

1. Look for executive or business coaches as opposed to career coaches (who excel in helping you find a job that fits you) or life coaches.

2. Look for someone who works with entrepreneurs, startup executives, or creative professionals as the majority of their clientele.

3. Look for someone who has experience working with lawyers and others in the legal industry.

4. Look for someone who gives you "homework" and holds you responsible for completing it.

 PRO TIP: If you've ever worked with a coach, you already understand how helpful they can be. Consider building the requirement for coaching for yourself into your job.

27

Advisory Boards

A greatly-underused resource for innovation programs is the advisory board. Advisory boards are a group of experts who provide advice, industry and customer knowledge, market awareness, subject matter expertise, and the like. They can work as sounding boards, a second pair of eyes, or get even more involved in strategic planning. They can also use their channels to publicize what you are doing. Most important, they open up their own personal networks to you and make key introductions.

Advisory boards can be made up of internal experts, external experts, or a combination of both. I favor the combination approach, ideally with a majority of external experts covering a wide range of key areas. Do not forget the voice of the customer.

You might meet monthly or quarterly by conference call (audio or video) and have at least one in-person meeting per year. Advisory board members are generally compensated, but there are many different ways in which this is done.

You are likely to consider advisory boards if you have a large or well-established program. However, an advisory board might provide even more value at the start of a new program or if you are contemplating a major change in direction or strategy.

For many people, just being asked to be on an advisory board is flattering. They will be receptive or let you know if they have conflicts and recommend others to serve in their places. In some cases, strategically adding an expert to your advisory board first might keep a competitor from adding that expert to their advisory board.

Advisory boards are under-utilized at this point, but offer the potential of first-mover and other advantages, especially from their industry knowledge and connections.

PRO TIP: Consider the creation of a small advisory board of internal and external experts as part of your pitch for your program or as part of your request for what you will need to take on the program.

PART IV

A TAXONOMY OF INNOVATION TOOLS

28

Scientific Method

L egal innovation professor Dan Linna has often said that many innovation and process improvement techniques are, at heart, just the scientific method. That observation has resonated with me since the first time I heard him say it. I want to lead off this section on innovation tools with the scientific method.

We might not remember much from the science classes of our youth, but it's likely that the scientific method is one of the things we do recall, at least fuzzily.

As a refresher, here's a brief statement of the Scientific Method from, as you might expect, the great explainer, Wikipedia.

"[The scientific method, which dates from at least the 17th century] involves formulating hypotheses, via induction, based on such observations; experimental and measurement-based testing of deductions drawn from the hypotheses; and refinement (or elimination) of the hypotheses based on the experimental findings."

Another way of describing it is to focus on the five components:

1. Asking a question;

2. Formulating a hypothesis;

3. Making a prediction;

4. Testing with experiments; and

5. Analyzing the results and deciding on next steps.

And an even simpler description:

1. Observation
2. Hypothesis
3. Prediction
4. Experiment
5. Conclusion.

There are other formulations, but those above will give you the gist of the method. For our purposes, I want to emphasize some key points that apply to a successful innovation program.

1. The importance of looking for gaps or problems to be solved and what job the customer needs to get done. Getting to the right question is extremely important.

2. We start with hypotheses or educated guesses that must be tested. We don't start by knowing the answer or the solution and then looking for the problem.

3. Our first attempt is just our first prediction of what the solution might be. There is a high likelihood that the first prediction will not be the final answer, nor should we expect it to be. We are looking for something to test.

4. Innovation is an experiment that takes place in the real world and we must thoroughly and honestly test our prediction.

5. Experiments generate results, they must be analyzed, and the results from the experiment (data) will determine our next steps and any necessary changes.

6. The scientific method is a process or cycle and the steps repeat as we continue to test our assumptions and hypotheses, and, perhaps, most important, as we examine whether we are even looking at the right question.

There is, in fact, method to the seeming madness of some innovation tools, as you will see in the following chapters in this Section of this book.

 PRO TIP: "It's just the scientific method" can be a powerful persuader of skeptics.

29

Experimentation, Results, and Failures

One more thing to keep in mind with the scientific method and innovation techniques is that, at heart, they create experiments. Experiments might be poorly designed, might be looking at the wrong question, might generate unexpected or negative results, or they might fail.

In a science lab, we would redesign, improve or change the experiment based on the results of the previous experiment. In innovation efforts, the same thing should happen. Getting good results is the "win," even if they aren't the results you expected or wanted. We learn, we refine, and we move forward. Some people like to call this "iteration."

Some experiments fail and some predictions are wrong. It's difficult, and it can be embarrassing, but we have to learn to live with that and treat it as a positive. In fact, part of the scientific method is trying to find an experiment in which your hypothesis fails. Keep that in mind. Failure is an option, and one that can move you forward.

 PRO TIP: Experiments give us data we can analyze and use for improvement. Stress test your hypotheses. If you don't, your customers will.

30

Feedback: Ask Your Customers

I f the definition of innovation includes the notion of increasing customer value (and it does), the definition of insanity must be running innovation programs that do not include, or severely limit, customer perspectives, insights, and feedback. I hope I don't need to say that twice.

However, the chair(s) at the table for customers (internal and external) are too often missing in meetings for all phases of the innovation process.

Why is this? It takes courage to ask your customers and hear their answers. It takes even more courage to ask them in person and hear what they have to say.

I've heard many lawyers give many reasons why they can't ask their clients for feedback. I've heard many clients give many reasons they can't give critical feedback to their lawyers. Many clients want their clients to ask them for feedback. And the non-virtuous cycle continues until the client, without warning or communication, simply moves the work to another firm. "Ghosting" is the popular term for that these days. This is one of the most puzzling disconnects in law practice.

Again, customer feedback is not a place where you need to re-invent the wheel. There are plenty of resources, templates, surveys and other tools readily available. Find something you like and try it. How simple can it be? The widely-used Net Promoter Score requires that a customer answer only two simple questions.

When you ask for customer feedback, act like you mean it and get back to the customer to discuss answers and overall results, where appropriate, and let them know about improvements you are making based on the feedback.

I've often participated in client feedback surveys and questionnaires. I'm hard-pressed to remember when there was actual follow-up. I assumed that someone had attended a seminar about client feedback, added it as an annual objective, and determined that "feedback theater" was good enough to check the box for that objective. And felt that was enough.

Did that encourage me to ever participate in the charade again? Not enough time in the day for that. Even one phone call would have made a difference and kept them from sliding onto my ghosting list. Either you care or you don't. It's pretty obvious.

Even worse are firms that schedule feedback calls and charge the client for the lawyer's time. NEVER do that. If you must, show it on the invoice as a write-off or a "no charge."

 PRO TIP: Find a simple feedback tool and start using it regularly. The old adage is correct: "Feedback is the breakfast of champions."

31

Brainstorming and Design Thinking

I wanted to start this section on innovation tools with the scientific method because science is often the last thing that comes to mind when someone walks into a room with post-it notes on the walls, crayons, tools, easels and whiteboards, and the assorted paraphernalia now associated with creativity events. However, the techniques underlying tools like brainstorming and design thinking have been studied and they bring results.

Let's first make a distinction between brainstorming and design thinking, at least for our purposes. I invite you to study them in more detail and find the definitions that feel most comfortable for you.

Brainstorming is an exercise intended to stimulate and record ideas from a group of people about a specific topic or question. (I might argue that mind mapping is a brainstorming technique for individuals, but that is a topic for another day.) Design thinking is a structured and sequential exercise, one of the steps of which is brainstorming, with the goal of reaching a hypothesis for solving a specific problem.

To me, brainstorming is part of design thinking, but brainstorming can be done without design thinking. Brainstorming is a single tool, while design thinking is a tool set.

If you are reading this book, you probably already know quite a bit about brainstorming and design thinking. You also probably participated in your share of these sessions. Therefore, I'll not go into detail of the basic concepts and approaches, but I will recommend reading the literature out there on their effectiveness and what works and what doesn't. You will find many great ideas to try.

Instead, I'll list some of my observations, insights, and tips about these kinds of events.

1. **Seeding.** A popular approach to brainstorming is to bring people into a room and hit them with a topic or ask them to start coming up with ideas. I now prefer a "seeded" approach in which you tell people ahead of time what the topic will be so ideas can start to incubate before the session begins.

   In one sense, it's a variation on the old exercise of "Imagine a polar bear in the corner of the room. Now try not to think of the polar bear." Consciously and subconsciously, your mind is starting to work in advance. It makes the voicing of ideas at the session easier.

   Similarly, I like asking people to start thinking of ideas in advance and jot them down. The approach can help jumpstart the momentum in the room because people can transfer notes to post-it notes at the beginning of the session.

2. **Give People Enough Time.** In one of my more radical opinions, I believe that most brainstorming sessions are too short and tend to reward people who think quickly as opposed to those who need to reflect, process, and take more time.

   I also believe that the best ideas come out at the end of a session, when people are starting to feel a little tired and impatient. I've even tried waiting until people have said that they are completely done, and then asking them to come up with "just one more" idea.

3. **Consider the Introverts.** A brainstorming session where people have to say their ideas aloud or where strong personalities dominate can be a disaster for introverts. In many cases, they will stop contributing ideas. Paying attention to the interplay of personality types can pay big dividends.

4. **Post-it Notes Really Can Be Magical.** Letting people write their ideas on post-it notes and stick them on the wall wherever they want takes some long strides toward addressing the introvert/extrovert issue mentioned in #3 above. Post-it notes also increase the number of ideas generated and eliminate discussion, organization, and editing of ideas at too early a stage. In many ways, using post-it notes democratizes and equalizes. They can also be collected at the end, transcribed, made available, and used again. Many wins, for a small cost. Remember to have enough writing tools.

5. **Enforce the "No Criticism" Rule**. A friend of mine has the greatest brainstorming session story I've ever heard. At the start of the session, the facilitator went through all the rules, emphasizing that all ideas are good, no one should criticize any idea, and that you should think as "out of the box" as possible. My friend took the rules seriously. She offered up an idea and the top executive in the company literally blurted out, "That's the stupidest idea I've ever heard." That's a true story. The idea was actually a very good one that deserved exploration, but you won't be surprised to learn that exactly zero other people else offered any ideas even close to her idea for the rest of the session.

I usually challenge people that, if they think an idea is stupid, to determine why they think it is stupid, and come up with a better idea and offer it.

6. **There Are Techniques to Avoid with Lawyers.** It's hard for me to imagine a harder group to work with in these types of sessions than lawyers. The number of quirks that you will find is unbelievable. Just a few things that will raise difficulties that I've seen: any kind of drawing exercise, any mention of the word "improv," using crayons, letting people put post-it notes wherever they want and not in any form of strict organization, offering pens in ink colors other than blue or black, and even more. Keep it simple. Brainstorming is a foreign concept for most lawyers, even though many of them use it without realizing it when working on case strategies or negotiations. Ease them into it in non-threatening ways.

7. **Defer Organization.** There is something about a wall of unorganized, uncategorized post-it notes that drives many lawyers crazy. They want to group, categorize, and collect. I will fight them on this and comfort them by promising that they will indeed get the chance to do all that in the next segment of the session. I also acknowledge that organizing and grouping is something that lawyers excel at and they will get the chance to show those skills later. Sometimes, that works, but organization is a powerful impulse for groups of lawyers.

8. **Diversity Matters.** Diversity is such a core part of innovation that I wrote a separate chapter (Chapter 11) on it. A lack of diversity makes for less interesting results and may cause you to miss key issues, problems, and approaches altogether. Again, I'll point you to Car-

oline Criado Perez's book, *Invisible Women*, to see some of the issues that arise out of leaving women out of the design process. A big diversity element most sessions miss: customers and clients.

9. **Make it a Competition.** Make a big goal, like 500 ideas. Divide people in teams and give small prizes to those on the team that creates the most ideas. I've also used "shark tank" pitch competitions and other competitive approaches at the end of design thinking sessions to encourage people to pull ideas together into pitches. Many types of game elements will help these sessions.

10. **Get People Out of Their Comfort Zones.** These sessions work best outside the day-to-day office and in locations and rooms suited to the purpose. Lots of open wall space, high ceilings, and the like. There is good research out there and lots of good recommendations. Dedicated innovation spaces can be a good choice.

11. **Agree to Action Steps and Acknowledge Effort.** It's no secret that many brainstorming and design thinking events do not result in anything actually being moved forward. I have a list of great ideas from events I've participated in that have died at the session or even showed up years later in press releases for new products from someone not involved in the events. I like to start events with a promise that some of the "winning" ideas will get added to the priority agenda for the year, and invite people to hold the organizers to that promise. Never ever forget to thank people for their ideas, energy, insights, time, and effort.

12. Follow Up. Get feedback from participants about the event and how it worked for them. Do they have suggestions for improvement? Would they like to participate in other sessions on this topic or other topics? Would they recommend that others participate in a similar event? Do they have other topic ideas? Would they like transcribed copies of the post-it notes? What would they like to see result from the session in 3 months, 6 months, or a year?

PRO TIP: Develop your own brainstorming style, experiment and see what works best for you and your groups, and keep people informed about what gets developed out of the session. Ongoing engagement is a priority goal.

32

Prototypes

As I mentioned in Chapter 32, the results of far too many ideation events is that the ideas are left at the event and abandoned. The question becomes what should be the first next step that is both concrete and practical?

Fortunately, the answer to the question is easy: a prototype.

As a starting point, Wikipedia is once again useful. A prototype is "an early sample, model, or release of a product built to test a concept or process or to act as a thing to be replicated or learned from." You can obviously dive much deeper into the topic (and Wikipedia lists six different categories of prototypes), but this definition is good enough.

Some key points:

1. **Early.** The prototype happens very early in the process. I like Tendayi Viki's observation on a recent webcast I attended that "a piece of paper can be a prototype." The piece of paper , of course, needs to have some writing or drawings on it. For example, a drawing of what a mobile app screen might contain is a simple prototype. Animations, models, and mockups would be more complex examples.

2. **Sample, model or release of a product.** A prototype involves compromises on what goes in and what stays out, and should never be thought of in terms of a finished product. In comparison, a "minimum viable

product" (MVP), to me, happens at a later stage than a prototype does.

3. **Built to test a concept or process.** Echoes of the scientific method. Experimentation and testing are primary goals of building a prototype.

4. **Or act as a thing to be replicated or learned from.** We learn, we incorporate the learnings into a new prototype, we learn some more, and we iterate until we have something that is mature and evolved enough to be tested as a product rather than a prototype.

One of the biggest hurdles in the innovation process is breaking out of the "ready, aim, aim, aim, aim, maybe fire" loop and moving to a "ready enough, aim, fire, check results, recalibrate, and iterate" model.

How do you create prototypes? Some organizations hire or engage artists and designers. On rare occasions, you find someone on your team with a knack for this: perhaps an artist or someone who has a robotics" or "maker" hobby. There are some consulting services that help with this phase of innovation.

In an example that I'm familiar with because I'm on the company's advisory board, FoundationLab (www.foundationlab.co) offers a monthly prototyping subscription service where you submit ideas ready for prototyping and they create developable prototypes for you. Not a service for everyone, but it might fit your needs. A side benefit of such a subscription service, after a year, if you are diligent, you will be able to show your management a dozen prototypes, and probably have several being far enough along to be in testing with customers.

Especially in the first year of your program, prototyping is essential to create momentum and show results. It must be in your innovation workflows.

 PRO TIP: Find a form of prototyping that best suits your style and needs and identify who can build those prototypes for you. Remember that a piece of paper can be a prototype.

33

MVPs

For me, the next step after prototypes is the "minimum viable product" or "MVP" phase. If you work with businesspeople in the world of products or innovation, MVP is an acronym or buzzword you will hear a lot.

The notion of MVP is associated with Eric Reis's book, *Learn Startup*. It falls into the experimentation and testing category of tools. An MVP is a version of your intended product that has just enough (or just barely enough) features and finish that you can put it into customers' hands without embarrassment and then get feedback from your customers to let you know what you did right, what you did wrong, and what to do next.

With MVPs, the customer feedback is likely to be direct and sometimes harsh. MVPs are not for the faint of heart. If feedback were a sport, MVPs would definitely be a contact sport. If used well, however, you can accelerate product development and potentially gain loyal customers and referrals at the same time.

Did I mention that this approach is not for the faint of heart? I recently thought I had a great idea that got crushed by potential customers before I even made it to the MVP stage. However, I'm happy to learn that sooner rather than later.

In comparison to prototypes, MVPs are more developed, more finished, and more like an actual product. If you think of the software world and the various phases of software releases (early developer release ("alpha"), beta releases, last pre-releases, and official product releases), MVPs probably fall somewhere in or before the beta release phase.

MVPs, because they are designed for getting feedback, must include a variety of ways to get that feedback back to you. And you need to act on the feedback and iterate new versions quickly. For this reason, MVPs work well with cloud-based tools and services.

A core principle of MVPs is that it is better to know than not to know, and to know sooner rather than later.

 PRO TIP: Consider the MVP approach when you have a product or service that is "close to done "but has been languishing in the finalization process.

34

Visual Tools: Canvases, Maps and Kanban Boards

---

n my own innovation journey, I've grown to like and rely on visual tools, like canvases and maps. I also use these tools in the law school innovation and technology classes I teach, and with others for whom and with whom I work. They are simple and effective ways to focus, collect, organize, and display your thinking. They also focus you on the most important and difficult questions.

In this chapter, I'll mention a few of the most common tools. As an innovator, you will want to know each of these tools well and to be able to communicate in the language of these tools.

Mind Mapping

Mind mapping is a tool I've used for more than 35 years to get ideas out of my head and on to paper (or, increasingly, into digital formats) and to organize those ideas once I see them. Most of my articles and presentations started out as mind maps, as did this book. Mind mapping was popularized by Tony Buzan in the 1970s, but some claim its origins stretch back to the Middle Ages. Buzan also described mind mapping as radiant thinking, which is helpful in understanding it. By the way, if your mind works best in the form of outlines, you will probably be doing most of what mind mapping does in outlines.

The concept is that you start by writing your central idea, problem, question, or topic in the center of the page. Then, using shapes, drawings, lines, and areas, you radiate the ideas in your idea around the central topic. There's a good illustration of this at https://en.wikipedia.org/wiki/Mind_map.

I find mind mapping to be a useful personal tool and a good introduction to the power of visual tools.

Value Proposition Canvas

Several of the most powerful visual innovation tools are associated with Alex Osterwalder. The simplest is the Value Proposition Canvas ("VPC"), and Osterwalder has written a book about it. There are also many videos available that illustrate how to use the tool.

There are only six components to this canvas or map. The page is divided into two parts (left side and right side) and there are three subparts on each side.

The goal of the VPC is to map the customers need in very personal practical terms to your product or service and what it provides to them. The comparison is illuminating. A VPC is useful in the earliest stages, as a way to consider new features, or as a way to evaluate a current effort. I find that it is increasing my "go to" tool. In my "Delivering Legal Services" class at Michigan State, it serves as the basis for much of what we do.

You can learn about the VPC in 3.5 minutes at https://www.strategyzer.com/canvas/value-proposition-canvas.

Nonetheless, I will explain it in this section.

On the right side of the page is a circle with three slices.

1. **Customer Job(s).** At the heart of the VPC is a focus on the customer and learning exactly what job the customer needs to get done. This approach grows out of Clayton Christensen's Jobs to Be Done theory (which I love).

Here, you want to learn exactly what job the customer wants to get done. It's similar to problem to be solved, but I think that looking at *jobs* gets you further into the solution. Often, I might think that I have a problem, but part of that is simply because I don't understand the job I need to do.

A quick example. My problem might be that my license plate will expire in two days. The job to be done is getting to the Bureau of Motor Vehicles office with the right documents in the next two days. The difference is subtle, but looking at the job helps you understand what the solution should look like and opens the door to any number of options.

2. Pains (to be relieved).

Next, we look at what pains the customer wants to relive or eliminate by completing the job. It's important to focus on the personal as well as the business pains. What makes someone cringe or wake up in the middle of the night? If a general counsel dreads the next executive committee because they know that they will be made fun of for not having simple metrics numbers at hand, then something that eliminates that dread will be far more attractive to them than something that predicts a possible 5% productivity increase.

3. Gains desired.

In one sense, gains can be thought of as the flip side of pains, but it's more complex than that. To use the previous example, if the gain the GC might desire is to be taken seriously as an equal business partner at the table. Other examples of gains might be meeting key personal objectives or improving metrics in excess of the targeted amount. Do not underestimate the importance of obtaining a promotion or even just keeping a job.

Next, we move to the left side of the page.

1. **Your proposed product or service offering.**

   In many ways, this segment of the canvas will be the easiest part. All you need is a short summary description of your product or service. For example, "keynote presentation on key legal innovation tools that really work."

2. **Pains alleviated.**

   What pains do you think that your offering in its current form will alleviate for your customer? I suggest listing at least three pains here. Ideally, don't look at the pains listed on the right side of the page yet.

3. **Gains achieved.**

   What gains do you expect that your customer will achieve from using your offering in its current form? Again, start with at least three gains.

If you just stopped here, you would have been able to summarize your customer research from the perspective of the customer, understand at a personal level what pains and gains they care about, very briefly describe your offering, and understand what pains and gains your offering addresses. Not a bad result from a one-page exercise.

However, the beauty of the VPC is the next step: matching up the pains lists and the gains lists. One of the biggest ways to fail in any product offering is to create something that your customers do not want or need, even if you do a great job of creating it.

This matching exercise will tell you if you are even close to being on the right track, suggest early course corrections, and reveal where you are relying on unverified assumptions and need more data.

As I said early, it's difficult for me to conceive of attempting any new offering, including this book, without using a value proposition canvas.

Business Model Canvas

Alex Osterwalder and his team at Strategyzer also developed a more complete mapping or canvas tool called the Business Model Canvas. An example can be found at https://www.strategyzer. com/canvas/business-model-canvas, along with a video that will help you learn the basics in two minutes. I recommend going beyond the video and reading *Business Model Generation*, by Alex Osterwalder and Yves Pigneur. I have made this book a required text for my Entrepreneurial Lawyering class at Michigan State University.

The business model canvas has nine boxes for you to fill in:

1. **Value Proposition.** If you use the VPC, and I recommend that you do, you can port your key points from the VPC into this box. You want to be able to explain and clearly state what value you provide to your customers and what pain and gain you address.

2. **Customer Segments.** Who are the target customers? What customers want or will receive the value you are offering? In many cases, there is a misalignment between who receives the value and who you believe the customer is. Also, who are your most important or key customers?

3. **Customer Relationships**. What type of relationships do customers in your segment expect from providers? Can you fulfill those expectations and what is the cost of doing so?

4. **Channels.** How do your customers want to be reached? Are you already reaching those customers? What are the most cost-effective of the customer-preferred channels to reach your customers?

5. **Key Activities.** What do you need to do to deliver your value proposition to your customers? How do you distribute the offering? What activities will generate revenue?

6. **Key Resources.** What resources (people, capital, et al.) will be required to bring your value proposition to your customer and enable your key activities?

7. **Key Partners.** What key partners will you be relying on? Will you need partners to perform key activities or deliver key resources? Who does what when and how?

8. **Cost Structure.** What are your most important expenses? What key activities and key resources are the most expensive?

9. **Revenue Streams.** Are customers will to pay for the value you bring (or some portion of it) and at what price? What are the paying for this value now or are they not doing it or paying anything? What do they want to pay? How will they be paying you? How much revenue do you expect from the offering and what portion of your organization's total revenue will that be?

If you work diligently on a business model canvas, it is a powerful tool. It forces you to address hard questions in a systematic, practical, and organized way. A good business model canvas will also make it easy for you to explain your offering and answer key questions from decision-makers about it. More than anything, it will help you demonstrate to decision-makers that you are prepared.

In many ways, I prefer the business model canvas to a standard business plan, but a completed business model canvas can be converted to a traditional business plan format if you are asked to provide one.

Lean Canvas

The lean canvas is similar to the business model canvas, but it incorporates lean and Toyota-based concepts. If you (or your organization) uses lean principles and methods, the lean canvas might appeal to you.

The lean canvas was created by Ash Maurya as a response to the business model canvas. It also tracks Eric Reis's lean startup methodology (see Chapter 34 on MVPs).

Key differences include a focus on "problem" and solution," a few more categories, and surfacing key metrics and early adopters.

I like using both canvases, but use the business model canvas first and then, later, compare the lean canvas I put together. As always, your goal is to find what tool works best for you.

Other Canvases

Canvas have become standard tools and there are other examples. Strategyzer is currently working on an innovation portfolio canvas. Others have tried to improve or customize canvases for certain industries or offerings. There are also "mission" canvases and canvases for non-profits. Do some experimentation.

Assumption Mapping

Assumption mapping gives you a way to surface your assumptions, sort them, and determine your product direction.

First, you do an exercise where you capture your assumptions on post-it notes and place them on a quadrant chart. The four quadrants are "known and important," "known and unimportant," "unknown and important," and "unknown and unimportant."

In the second phase, you will use those assumptions to create three categories: (1) **Desirability** (do customers want this?), (2) **Feasibility** (can we build it?), and (3) **Viability** (should we do this?). You then turn those categories into circles in a Venn diagram. You will use the Venn diagram to see what insights are revealed, especially in the section where the three circles overlap.

Maps and other visual tools are powerful ways to plan and explain your efforts using an engaging and thorough structure. Find one or two that you like and seem to work for you.

 PRO TIP: Require the completion of a value proposition canvas for any proposed new effort.

35

Metrics, KPIs and OKRs

I f we had a list of modern proverbs, we'd certainly find "what gets measured gets done" on the list. If not, another variation, "what gets measured gets managed" would take its place.

Many lawyers like to say that they went to law school to avoid taking math classes. Creative types don't like to be measured or believe that what they do best can't be measured in traditional ways. For example, in six minutes, I might have three ideas. The first saves the organization a million dollars in costs. The second brings in a million dollars of new revenue. The third becomes the longtime example in the organization of how bad an idea can be. In a billable hours setting, the value of that work is measured at 0.1 hours. Period.

Let me now adjust the adage slightly to "what gets meaningfully measured gets done." This one-word change leads us into the world of metrics, KPIs (key performance indicators), and the newer term, OKRs (objectives and key results). A great introduction to all of these concepts, especially OKRs, is John Doerr's book, *Measure What Matters*. Tom Mighell and I also discussed all of these concepts, their interrelatedness, and how they are and might be used in the legal industry in a podcast titled "Best Practices for Measures and Metrics in Law Firms" at https://legaltalknetwork.com/podcasts/kennedy-mighell-report/2019/02/best-practices-for-measures-and-metrics-in-law-firms/.

The most useful distinction for me is that measures give you one piece or type of data (e.g., billable hours) and metrics give you a ratio or relationship between two pieces or types of data (e.g., billable hours per month). You can have measures without metrics, but not metrics without measures. There is no need to make it any more complicated than that.

No matter how math-averse you think you are, you will see that there are many measures and metrics in everything that you do in innovation. Post-it notes per session, prototypes per year, new employees added per year, comparisons to budget targets, and much, much more.

I've always gotten a chuckle when people say, "we need some metrics" or "let's find some metrics." Metrics are right there in front of you. The point is to find the metrics that matter to you, and to keep re-evaluating them. I'll end with a few metrics at the end of this chapter that I like these days. You are welcome to use them as starting points, but the better approach would be to challenge them, see if they apply to your effort, and decide what matters for you.

You can use metrics as targets or goals. For example, you might want to create one prototype per month.

You can also use metrics for comparison. For example, in one brainstorming session, you harvested 250 ideas. In another, you harvested 500 ideas. You also know that your average is 400 ideas per session.

You can also track results on a standard basis to help you communicate succinctly to others what is happening. For example, in 2018, you had six client pilot projects. In 2019, it's up to fifteen pilots, including new pilots for four of the six 2018 clients. Decision-makers can understand those numbers.

The question then becomes, if there are many possible metrics, which ones are the most important?

Key Performance Indicators (KPIs)

A key performance indicator is a measurable, quantifiable value that helps you track your progress toward your most important business goals. There are plenty of examples, including the list of 136(!) KPIs at https://www.scoro.com/blog/key-performance-indicators-examples/.

Practicing lawyers know all too well that their KPI too often is simply billable hours per year. If you are only in the business of selling hours, that might be a good KPI, but it does not provide as much information as other related KPIs (such as ratio of billable hours to billed hours to collected hours, profitability, impact on profits per partner, ratio of compensation to collected hours, and the like) do.

A good KPI allows you to have the data necessary to set and track goals and objectives. For example, an important KPI for many companies is the average acquisition cost of a new customer. If you find that the cost per acquired customer is $100, then you can see what it would take to drive that cost down to $80 and set a goal of reducing the average acquisition cost to $80 in a year. You might also dig deeper into what customers are the outliers (much higher cost or much lower cost) and make a decision to adjust your sales efforts accordingly.

As a general matter, you want a handful of useful KPIs. You might adjust them from time to time, but tracking the same KPIs over several years will show trends and give you other important insights.

Objectives and Key Results (OKRs)

Sometimes, an organization will track KPIs, but there are no consequences for not achieving results or making improvements. Have you ever been part of a community organization that tracks new memberships and watched each year as the numbers go down and no changes are made in leadership or methods?

OKRs are credited to Andrew Grove at Intel and are now used by Google and other leading technology companies. As I mentioned, the best resource on OKRs is John Doerr's book, *Measure What Matters*.

In simplest terms, OKRs take KPIs and turn them into objectives. People know whether they have met the objective or not. There are consequences of not meeting your OKRs. And they are checked on a fast cycle, often quarterly.

If you are not meeting your OKR, it will be made visible early in the process. It can then be looked into, and adjusted, if necessary. Or it will have a negative impact on your performance evaluation.

OKRs are a new trend, and the idea of OKRs can make people uncomfortable, especially if consequences are not evenly enforced or employees perceive favoritism. Another danger is that people lobby for OKRs that will be easy for them to achieve.

However, tying personal and team objectives to KPIs and making them OKRs is an attractive approach.

Some Innovation KPIs

With the caveats that you should create your own KPIs and I lean more to quantity than quality, which you might disagree with, here are a few KPIs I like.

1. Client conversations per year

2. Prototypes created per year

3. Innovation presentations (internal and external), including RFP and panel convergence presentations, made per year

4. Average cost of new customer acquisition

5. New pilots per year

6. Return customers (new projects from previous clients) per year

7. External mentions of client projects per year

8. Number of client-initiated meetings per year

9. Revenues per year

10. Savings per year

11. New business won where client indicated that innovation efforts were an important factor in their decision per year

12. Employee turnover on team per year

13. Inquiries from other organization employees to join team per year

14. Number of ideas per ideation session

15. Number of management meetings head of innovation effort attended per year

Depending on the type of effort, I would pick three to five of these that made the most sense as my KPIs, but I'd track, at least on an informal or shadow basis, many of the others.

Again, you want to find KPIs that best fit your efforts, your vision and mission, and the results you want to achieve. All of your KPIs will help you with internal selling to management and make the case for your future plans and budgets.

 PRO TIP: Take the initiative in recommending KPIs, get agreement from management on those KPIs, and provide regular, one-page, reports on KPI success.

36

Processes and Process Improvement

In my informal surveys and my experience, lawyers tend to be about 10% (or less) idea people and about 90% process people. While I prefer innovation efforts to focus on creating value for customers and developing new business models, it's inevitable that many legal innovations will fall into the "process improvement" or "optimization" category. And that's OK. Sustaining innovations are important.

In this chapter, I want to touch on two popular and important process improvement methodologies and some mapping techniques associated with these approaches that you might find helpful. There are other process improvement methodologies (six sigma, lean six sigma, theory of constraints, and others) and, by not including them, I'm not downplaying their importance in the right situation, but I don't want to discuss all of them. You will want to do your own exploration. For example, I'm fascinated by theory of constraints and something known as the OODA loop, which I don't talk about in this book at all.

However, I want to focus on what seem to be the two big ones today: Lean and Agile. Both come from outside law. Lean comes out of the manufacturing world (and, more specifically, is associated with Toyota) and Agile arose out the software world. There has been some effort to apply these methodologies to services businesses (including law), with mixed success.

On an organization-wide basis, these approaches would be difficult to apply, but, for innovation efforts, they offer much potential and should be considered, especially if you or members of your team have a background or experience in either of the methods. If you go this route, you must get a strong commitment from management to fund the necessary education and training, and understand how much commitment and work will be involved.

Lean

Lean grew out of quality improvement methods pioneered by Toyota. I'm glossing over some nuances here but Lean is sometimes referred to as the "Toyota Way" and has a rich history. "Kaizen" is another word you will see in this context. It does have its own language, including a system of belts of different colors.

In simplest terms, lean is about the elimination of waste through customer-focused continuous improvement. There's a lot to unpack in that sentence.

In the standard definition, lean has six core principles:

- ► Focus on delivery of customer value
- ► Respect and engagement for workers
- ► Improve value by eliminating waste
- ► Maintain system flow
- ► "Pull" more important than "push"
- ► Strive for perfection continuously

Hundreds of books and courses, many by leading practitioners, have been written on lean, so there are many places to learn more about lean. Outside of manufacturing, this method has had great success in hospitals. In just one example, hospitals have dramatically reduced infection rates by focusing on hand washing and other simple sanitary techniques. In the Resources chapter, I have listed some of the lean resources I like and many of them will walk your through the considerations and steps you need to create a lean approach.

Agile

The Agile method arose from the world of software development in reaction to the tradition "waterfall" development approach. In waterfall, you work at the front end to create a complete list of specifications and requirements, set milestones, and follow the plan to completion. As the pace of technological change and customer expectations accelerated, the inflexibility and timeframes (often more than a year, and several years in large projects) caused major issues, delays, failed projects, delivery of something that the customer no longer wanted, and budget over-runs. Worse yet, there was a period of acceptance testing that had to happen at the end where problems, sometimes major, had to be located and corrected.

In Agile, the focus turns to flexibility, customer engagement, and moving faster to delivery of what made the most sense for the customer at the actual time of release. Testing and bug fixing happen on an ongoing basis. If parts of the project are finished, they can be released separately and early to get customer feedback. The Agile approach is often used today in mobile applications and web-based (or cloud) services.

Agile comes with its own insider vocabulary (sprints, scrums, scrum masters, story points, to name a few) that can be off-putting. Many organizations do not like to trade certainty (especially about costs and performance specs) for flexibility. However, Agile has increased in popularity in the last several years especially, and a few different variations on the standard approach has evolved.

Agile divides a project into focused two-week "sprints." Each sprint is focused on a story. There are very short "stand up" meetings called "scrums" that happen every day so everyone can learn what is going on with others, what dependencies are still outstanding, and the like. Customer or user input is included. At the end of each sprint, a new sprint happens based on the results of the previous sprints and this continues until the project is completed.

You should be able to see how the Agile method could work well in innovation efforts, if you commit to it. As an aside and as a freebie to readers, I've long felt that a great innovation project would be to create an Agile approach template for lawyers working on big business deals like mergers and acquisitions.

Mapping and Other Visual Tools

In the world of lean especially, there are some useful visual and mapping tools. I want to highlight three of them.

1. **Process Maps.** Process maps are forms of flow charts that help you visualize in one place all of the parts of a process. They can be useful obtaining agreement on what the process actually is, bringing new people up to speed, and surfacing extra steps or duplication.

2. **Value Stream Maps.** Value stream maps can be thought of as process maps on steroids. They can be immensely detailed and are focused on finding, measuring, and reducing or eliminating waste. They are not for the faint of heart, but if you have someone on your team who is good at them, it's easy to see how useful they might be in certain projects.

3. **Kanban Boards.** Kanban boards are part of my personal tool set these days. I used them in writing this book. In a way, they are visual to-do lists, but they also show flow and what has been done.

A simple kanban board might have three columns: Ready, Doing, and Done. It might be a white board where you use dry erase markers or a board where you use a post-it note for each task. I favor a five-column approach: Backlog, Ready, Doing, Waiting (for someone else), and Done.

Once you have your tasks in the proper categories, you work only on what's in the Doing column, and move things to the Done column when finished. As a space opens in the Doing column (or as a priority changes), you move a task from Ready to Doing.

Kanban boards give you a simple dashboard for your work on a project. I prefer a large whiteboard, but there are online tools like Trello that allow you to create digital Kanban boards. I especially like that the "Done" items stay in view, giving you a sense of accomplishment.

I've added the "Backlog" and "Waiting" categories based on some modified templates I found. "Backlog" lets me see what is coming down the road that I want to keep in mind. "Waiting" lets me know that I have something currently in someone else's hands that might come back to me or I might need to follow-up on.

You have a process in place, whether you realize it or not. It's important to know that there are some approaches that have become industry standards that you might adopt or adapt to your own processes or that you can use in process improvement innovation projects.

 PRO TIP: Get a decent knowledge of the standard process improvement methods and try to become well-versed in the one that appeals to you.

37

Product and Project Management

———————

I n this chapter, I want to cover a few management and systems approaches: project management, product management, change management, and systems thinking. Again, I've chosen to highlight just a few of these approaches.

As is my continuing theme, much has been written about all aspects of the innovation process and you do not want to spend a lot of time reinventing or re-creating techniques that are already well-known outside the legal world. I've picked the four I consider most important. If you forced me to pick one as the most important for most readers, I'd pick change management.

Project Management

It's difficult for me to conceive how a large innovation project can be successful without a trained project manager. In my time at Mastercard, I had the good fortune of working with some great project managers. A good project manager makes sure things get done on time, holds people accountable, and probably does a million things that no one appreciates. My favorite project managers got commitments from people and called them out if they didn't meet those commitments.

There are educational programs, certification programs, and training for project managers. It's not something to pick up and learn from a "for Dummies" book and hit the ground running. A great project manager is worth her weight in gold. If you find one, do everything you can to keep her. Unfortunately, these are the people your customers are most likely to hire away from you.

Product Management

If you plan to be creating products, especially commercial products, you will want to know about product management and product managers. This category is much different from project management.

The focus here is on everything it takes to bring a product to market, make it successful in the market, and help develop the roadmap for the product.

Change Management

Innovation is about change. Change management is a whole field that has grown up to help us learn the impact of change and how best to deal with its many impacts. For example, change usually meets resistance. There is much research on this topic and approaches that can work for you. My advice is to make learning about change management an education priority.

Systems Thinking

We work in so many silos these days. It's easy to forget that a change in your space can have many consequences in other areas that are part of an extended system. If a lawyer adopts documentation automation tools to draft documents but does not factor in its impact on time-based billing or minimum billable hours requirements, there will be unexpected consequences.

Many people think of innovation as its own separate field. It's easy to become just another silo. There is a bigger picture.

The field of systems thinking addresses the interplay of systems. Much has been written on this topic, but my favorite starting point is still Peter Senge's classic book, *The Fifth Discipline: The Art & Practice of The Learning Organization*, which I revisit every few years.

These tools and approaches will give you a better grounding in both theoretical and practical approaches around innovation and delivering results. As a side effect, they are also likely to help you improve your own innovation game. And learning about them will help you stand on the shoulders of innovation giants.

 PRO TIP: Include space on your team and a line in your budget for at least one project manager.

38

Advanced Techniques: Sprints and Labs

There are two advanced tools that I want to highlight in this chapter: design sprints and innovation labs. My insights and perspective come in no small part from my time as in-house counsel for Mastercard Labs, Mastercard's innovation laboratory.

These tools generally will make sense for large organizations with a significant budget, commitment, and vision. It would be easy to burn up a lot of money doing these techniques wrong or even just partially right.

On the other hand, they tangibly demonstrate serious commitment to innovation and offer ways to focus on customer problems (think pains and gains) and customer value. Based on my experience, these techniques can become key differentiators in outside firm panel selection RFPs and similar contexts. They also require that customers be further along the innovation curve than simpler techniques do.

It should be no surprise that I like both of these techniques. A lot.

Design Sprints

Design sprints come in several flavors, but most techniques owe a major debt of gratitude to the Google design sprint approach set out in the book, *Sprint: How to Solve Big Problems and Test New Ideas in Just Five Days,* by Jake Knapp, John Zeratsky, and Braden Kowitz.

The book offers a recipe and structure for creating and running a five-day design sprint offering that is repeatable, focuses on customer problems, and produces a functional prototype at the end. My advice is that, if you are interested in learning about design sprints or offering them, start by reading *Sprint*.

Others have made adjustments or what they believe to be improvements to the standard approach, most often in the form of the prototype deliverable at the end of the process. In fact, Google has recently made some changes to the original process that will be documented in a new edition to the book.

The most common reservations about design sprints are the time required and the difficulty of getting key players together in the same room at the scheduled time. FoundationLab (of which I am on the advisory board), for example, shortened its design sprint offering to four days, focused on getting more pre-work done in advance, and tailored the offering to the legal industry.

Design sprints are a big offering and the decision to offer them to your customers is a big one as well. Despite the risk, the return on tying customers to you by solving the problems they bring to you can be very high.

One piece of advice: if you want to offer design sprints, at least be invested in the idea enough that you use your own design sprint process to create your design sprint offering. If someone tells me about their design sprint offering, I love to ask whether they used their own method to create it. I don't like to see any hesitation in the answer to that question.

Labs

I once had a client who constantly referred to his business and his vision of it as the "big enchilada." An innovation lab is a big enchilada.

Innovation labs are already taking many forms, but, at the core, they involve a separate internal or external organization wholly devoted to innovation, usually in one or just a few forms. The level of commitment is immense, but an innovation lab shows your customers a high level of commitment.

Labs take vision. They take champions. They take an unflinching focus on providing customer value. They challenge priorities and assumptions. They provide a testing ground for the future. And they can be a source of entirely new business models and revenue streams.

There is no cookie cutter approach or "one-size-fits-all" template. You'll need to use everything in this book and more to get an innovation lab off the ground and make it successful. If you are willing to take on that challenge, I salute you and hope this book stands you well on your journey.

 PRO TIP: Dream big.

39

Other Innovation Tools and Techniques

———————

You can explore the magical world of innovation tools and find many treasures. In this chapter, I want to encourage you do that, point out a few directions, and end with a tool I've found especially intriguing.

How can you continue to innovate without innovating for yourself, your team, and your program? That question has always answered itself for me. The best innovation tool is continuous learning.

There are so many great education resources about innovation now available. Books, podcasts, articles, and presentation slides. Some of the most-respected design and innovation firms in the world offer free webinars and videos. There are also courses, bootcamps, intensive sessions, and the like. There are conferences, groups to join, and so much more. There is a growing number of people working in legal innovation who are creating their own communities.

There is no need to go it alone. Take advantage of what is available. I wrote this book to share with you what I've learned and to help start a community of interest. Help me do that.

Let me end with one tool I've become especially intrigued by. It's from William Duggan's book, *Creative Strategy: A Guide for Innovation*. Duggan argues that some of the best innovation comes from adapting and combining techniques that have worked elsewhere. He advocated using a simple matrix to facilitate a simple three-step "rapid appraisal" process.

First, you "chunk" or break your problem into a set of smaller problems or components. Some call this process "decomposition." You place those problems on the vertical axis of your matrix.

Second, you look at other industries, geography, times, and the like to see if anyone, anywhere has created a solution to any of the smaller "problems" on your vertical axis that you can use or adapt to your problem. Those solutions go at the top of the matrix on the horizontal axis.

Third, for lack of a better term, you start slicing and dicing to find what interesting ideas come up at the intersections of problems and solutions.

The example I gave of my student who came up with a ride-sharing service for customers of an expungement clinic is a good example. He looked at an Uber or Lyft model, a gift or exchange model (if you get a free ride, you will be more willing to reciprocate by providing data), and built from there.

This matrix is an example of a simple visual tool that captures some standard approaches and helps you use them in fast and powerful ways.

 PRO TIP: Do not cut corners on your learning and insist that your employer facilitate your learning and your access to innovation communities.

PART V

EXAMPLES OF INNOVATION EFFORTS

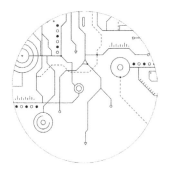

40

Three Innovation Efforts Corporate Counsel Want

This chapter contains some of my best insights from work on the customer side as an in-house counsel. It also contains some of my best practical advice on actual innovation projects. It's up to you to choose whether you want to follow this advice or not, but I urge you to consider it, especially as you get started and if you are considering only innovation megaprojects.

A few years ago, a survey of general counsels showed that the most common answer to the question "What innovation has your outside counsel brought you in the last year?" was "None." None. Note that I said most common because saying "most popular" answer would be wrong.

What's been striking in my career is how I often I hear about in-house counsel telling their outside firms exactly what they need and the outside firms either ignoring that or returning with something completely different.

The current fashion in innovation proposals is heavy on artificial intelligence, contract life cycle management, and the like. They propose big, expensive projects with lots of moving parts and many permissions and much coordination required in a corporate setting. More important, the benefits tend to be more theoretical than practical, and, truth be told, could often be achieved by using existing legal tech tools already on the market.

What do I think clients want and where you should consider focusing your efforts?

1. **Simple Dashboards**. Far too often, basic information needed by a general counsel or in-house counsel is simply not readily at hand in an easy-to-find and easy-to-consume way. Talk to any general counsel and you are likely to hear a story about them being asked by a CEO or CFO simple business questions like year-to-date legal spend, spend compared to budget, total legal exposure, law firms with highest spend, and other standard metrics (let alone key performance indicators), and not having any answer other than, at best, that they needed to have some reports run to get this basic information.

   Similarly, in-house counsel too often don't have metrics at hand that are useful to them: caseload, success rates, numbers of contracts signed, average times for projects, and the like.

   I often use the Thomson Reuters Legal Tracker (formerly known as Serengeti) as an example. It is probably the standard tool for managing outside counsel (and has been so for many years). However, I often point people to the simple and targeted dashboard tools designed around metrics they've learned that in-house counsel care about and want.

   Dashboards are a simple and powerful concept and the discussion around what should go into them will give you and your client tremendous insights into their needs, their approaches, and what is most important to them.

   Law departments are increasingly looking to outside counsel to recommend legal technology tools. You get at least as much credit for suggesting an existing tool (which the client might already own) to accomplish something valuable for the client as you will by creating a custom tool. If the only innovation offering you were bringing to corporate clients was help in creating effective Legal Tracker dashboards, you would go to the top of the class and open the doors to other innovation opportunities.

2. **Expert Locators.** People have been working on full-scale knowledge management platforms for many years. A big lesson is that they are very hard to do successfully and have them fully adopted by users.

   However, there is one aspect of knowledge management tools that can be broken out and used to create customer value. I use the term "expert locator." In any organization, we know that there are usually one or two people who are either the "right person" to answer a question or can point you to that person.

   Getting to that person is a hard-enough problem, but it becomes exponentially more difficult when you want to find experts with your organization and in your outside law firms.

   For example, if I need help on a blockchain legal question, I don't really want to go through the client representatives of my outside firms to find a lawyer with that expertise and experience. I'd like to find them quickly and talk to them directly.

   A tool that allows me to do that would be highly useful and appreciated, especially if it eliminates hype and puffery and can get me to the real experts. If that's an associate, that's fine with me. I have work to be done, and ego-feeding of law firm partners is not part of that work.

Expert locators are a highly fertile area for innovation efforts. You probably already are realizing that, if you create a tool, it can be repeated for other clients and even become a product.

3. **Lightweight KM Tools.** They are lots of skeletons on the road to the land of successful comprehensive knowledge management projects. They are hard work and, in some legal settings, impossible.

    In many law departments (and law firms), there are many ideas about desired, target knowledge tools: news and development mini-sites, clause repositories, negotiation playbooks, best practices, and even tips and after-action learnings.

    By reducing the scope of the project, your odds of achieving completion, results, and customer value increase greatly. The term for this is "addition by subtraction." I'll discuss in Chapter 46 something we did at Mastercard called the New Technologies Center of Excellence (the acronym was "NeTCoE") that illustrates this approach.

The key takeaway from this chapter is that you can focus on certain types or families of innovation efforts that are easy to explain, much simpler and faster to execute than big projects, and show value quickly. And, as I'm sure you have noticed, each generates the opportunity to learn about a client's business, needs, and problems in a deep way, bring value to the client, and cement your role as an innovative, helpful, trusted advisor, while giving you an opportunity to create something repeatable for other clients or potentially even a new product line.

That's a lot of wins.

 PRO TIP: Three places to find early wins if you are struggling to find a starting point: simple dashboards, expert locators, and lightweight knowledge management tools.

41

Selling to GCs and Other Decisionmakers

----

t's worth repeating that several years ago, a survey of general counsels asked what innovation their outside counsel had brought to them. The top answer was "none."

In one sense, the threshold for outside counsel innovation efforts is quite low and the opportunity to differentiate from other firms is there for the taking. In another sense, however, the answer illustrates the desire of in-house counsel to see their outside firms take the lead in innovation and technology initiatives and their disappointment with the perceived lack of leadership.

For in-house counsel, there is a sharp disconnect between what is requested and what outside firms seem to hear from them. In-house counsel often tell me about asking for simple email newsletters from outside counsel that, rather than summarize new cases or laws, offer a firm's perspectives and insights and suggest practical action steps. Then they say, "And we never got them."

A legal technology "solution" that outside counsel like to advocate is "contract lifecycle management." Yes, there is a need, but those projects are not at the top of the in-house priority list, are nightmarishly complex to implement, and involve many moving parts in the entire corporation.

If, instead, the innovation process produced a pilot project of one of the three simple ideas I suggested in Chapter 41 (i.e., a dashboard of highly relevant data, an expertise locator, or a list of places where routine legal review could be eliminated), you would have delighted in-house counsel. Each of these addresses pain points, solves business problems, and creates easy experiments. Each of these also illustrate how well you have listened and suggested some options that have worked elsewhere, not just tried to sell a pre-conceived innovation "solution." And they provide value to the client and help them get their jobs done.

Many lawyers hate to "sell." Most in-house counsel hate to be "sold to." The good news is that pitching innovation efforts should not involve selling in the classic sense. It should consist of many of your best lawyering skills: asking good questions, active listening, investigating, getting to the core problem, looking at options, and patience. You want to understand what the client wants before you jump in with a solution.

In the innovation process, there are three steps, as I have mentioned: why, what, and how. The sequence is to start with why, move to what, and, only at the very end, look at the how. Resisting the urge to move too quickly to the how stage plays a key role in success.

While there are many definitions of innovation, most of them emphasize "customer-focused" or "customer-centered" problem solving. Your client has the problem to solve. Your goal, and your role, are to help your client solve their problem and eliminate their pains and achieve their gains.

The client does not want you to swoop in and save the day. You can do that when handling important legal work. Instead, clients want to be the heroes of their own innovation stories. They want a guide with a plan to help them win the prize while avoiding disaster. Think Yoda, not Superman.

With that in mind, what approaches work best when discussing innovation projects or processes with a client?

1. **Bring it Up First.** Since outside firms are known for NOT bringing innovation ideas to corporate counsel, simply initiating the conversation might be a differentiator for you. If you put innovation in the context of

improving the relationship, controlling or cutting legal spend, or a new benefit for key clients, you will have a winning combination.

2. **Talk to the Real Decision-makers.** General counsel often lead and drive department innovation and select the winning projects to carry forward. However, they typically delegate the details to the innovation team. To move specific efforts forward, you will need to identify and engage with leadership of this team. We see more law departments with roles like Chief Innovation Officer than ever before.

3. **Use the Value Proposition Canvas.** A great, simple tool to use is something called the Value Proposition Canvas , described in more detail in Chapter 35. It gives you a quick, visual way to map out the client's problem, the pains the clients hope to alleviate or eliminate, and the gains they want to achieve. You can then match those items with the project or approach you suggest. For example, a client's problem might be that they don't know who the subject matter experts are for specific issues. The pains might include not knowing there was someone who could answer the question off the top of her head or mismatching people to projects. The hoped-for gains might be getting the right work to the right people or creating subject matter teams. After making the diagnosis, you can match the proposed solution (expert locator app) or process (design and prototyping sprint) and its pains solved and gains achieved with those desired and see how good the fit is.

4. **Pitch Pilots, Not Products.** Upwards of 90% of innovation projects fail or drastically change from the initial concept. That's a good thing. It's part of the innovation and start-up process. The more pilots, the better. Pilots

give you and the client prototypes to test, examples of possible projects to share with others, and quick wins that build momentum.

5. **Understand Internal Goals and Objectives.** In-house counsel and law departments have annual objectives and goals. Understand what those are and make the part of the equation. Visible achievement of annual goals will always be a desired gain for your client.

6. **Bring the Whole Team.** Get the right teams talking, especially in panel convergence presentations. If a law department has a Chief Innovation Officer or innovation lead, they will want to meet and talk with their counterparts. Your client will want to hear from the people who can answer their specific questions.

Innovation initiatives from outside counsel are moving quickly from nice-to-have to must-have. Law departments are looking for help to show innovation results and meet corporate and department goals and objectives. In-house counsel will be looking for guides who give them plans to achieve what they need and remain the heroes of their own stories. If you can provide that, you will cement long-term client relationship and open the doors to new legal work as a preferred law firm and a valued partner.

 PRO TIP: Persuading a general counsel on innovation efforts requires special approaches and language, but these can be learned.

42

Panel Convergence

S tories abound these days about general counsels wanting their outside law firms to help them with innovation and technology efforts. My own conversations indicate that the real wish goes a step further. General counsel want their outside firms to bring them measurable value with innovation and technology initiatives that align with their legal and, more importantly, business goals. Even a quick scan of recent survey results from Thompson Hine (https://www.thompsonhine.com/uploads/1135/doc/ClosingTheInnovationGapPrint.pdf) will have you agreeing with their assessment that there is an "Innovation Gap." Only 29% of participants said that their outside firms have brought them "significant" innovation.

Is it possible that an increasingly common practice in corporate law departments is a solution to achieving these innovation and technology goals?

Panel convergence (or, as I sometimes call it, panel consolidation) is now a popular approach in corporate law departments under pressure from CEOs and CFOs to gain control of legal spend. In some cases, making legal spend predictable and more certain can be more important than cost reduction, although fee discounting is commonly associated with panel convergence.

The concept is a simple. A legal department puts out a request for proposals ("RFP") for firms to pitch for a place on what will be a small and select list of approved outside law firms on the panel. Firms complete what tends to be a very long and complex questionnaire, firms are selected to present in person as part of a "beauty contest," and finalists are selected.

Only the firms on the new panel list are eligible to receive work from the law department. Not making the panel will have drastic consequences for outside law firms. In most, if not all, cases, the convergence effort results in a dramatic reduction in the number of outside firms used by the law department.

I like to trace the notion of convergence back to quality pioneer W. Edwards Deming, who believed that by reducing the number of outside suppliers (he went so far as to suggest getting it down to one) and working with them to get aligned on business goals, you could achieve excellent business results. In the legal profession, the Dupont Legal Model (http://businessoflawblog.com/2016/07/3-business-insights-learned-from-the-dupont-model/) and Jeff Carr's ACES model (https://remakinglawfirms.com/wp-content/uploads/2018/04/Univar-Guidelines-and-Procedures-for-Outside-Counsel.pdf) are examples of this approach.

Some of the overarching goals of a panel convergence effort are:

1. "Rationalizing" and "right-sourcing" legal service pro-viders (reducing number of firms and directing lawyers to the law firms (or, increasingly, alternative legal ser-vices providers) best suited for types of work)

2. Reducing or controlling costs, including discounts, flat fees, staffing changes, and alternative billing arrange-ments.

3. Creating long-term relationships with outside firms so they can understand the business and its goals and strategies.

4. Aligning outside firms with legal and business goals, objectives, strategies, and risk tolerance.

5. Maintaining consistent legal approaches

6. Incentivizing outside firms to bring new ideas, innovation, and value to the client

7. Addressing diversity and inclusion objectives.

8. Generating measurable value.

You can probably think of other goals as well.

The results of these efforts are mixed. Reducing the number of outside firms and achieving some kind of price discounting or cost control are probably the most common "wins." However, my friends in the legal pricing world often say that the discounts tend to be smallish and law firms increase hourly rates to adjust for the discounting.

Convergence efforts are difficult, time-consuming, and can raise all kinds of difficult issues, especially when longstanding outside firm relationships are put in jeopardy. The work on the finalization of the panel can be so difficult that the ongoing follow-up work of pursuing all the benefits of convergence is neglected. I talked to an in-house counsel who said that her law department hadn't updated the firms on the approved panel in fifteen years.

Other common benefits that seem to take effect are enforcement of entering into specific engagement letters, staffing directives, timing of invoicing, e-billing, and participating in outside counsel management systems.

However, the goals of business alignment, value generation, and innovation often get lost in the process, even though many outside panel RFPs specifically address these issues. Just like firms often answer that they do literally every type of legal work, law departments often let firms get away with saying that they are "great on innovation too."

In this chapter, I want to take an in-depth look at how panel convergence can, perhaps paradoxically, act as an innovation destroyer if not properly tended, how panel convergence should, if you follow good, often commonsense practices, act as an innovation driver, and suggest some practical action steps for you to consider.

Innovation Destroyer?

An observation, perhaps controversial. Panel convergence efforts do not achieve as much as they could because corporate legal departments do not appreciate the power that they have in what is now a buyers' market. In simplest terms, outside firms under competitive pressure to stay on a panel or gain access to a panel are more willing to negotiate than you might expect. It is a huge benefit for a firm to get on a panel. If a firm is not on a panel, it is often extraordinarily difficult to get the firm added at a later point. If BigLaw firms will not move enough for corporate law departments, many perfectly capable mid-market regional firms will do so. This buyers' market observation applies especially to innovation.

There are three points where panel convergence efforts can damage or destroy innovation goals:

1. RFP creation and solicitation of proposals;
2. RFP and innovation pitch evaluation; and
3. Maintenance and review of convergence effort.

RFPs

In too many cases, panel convergence RFPs for outside firms run into the hundreds of pages. Even the section on innovation or technology can be lengthy, not on point, and cobbled together from multiple sources. In the worst case, a law department might abdicate responsibility for the RFP language to the procurement or sourcing department.

I'm not sure that inhouse counsel needs to know much more at the RFP response stage than (1) what are examples of what a firm actually has done and are currently working on, (2) what would the firm plan to do specifically for the law department, (3) what people and infrastructure does the firm have for delivering innovation projects, and (4) what data demonstrates the firm's level of commitment to innovation? If I have answers to those questions, I can probably make a decision about whether a firm passes the initial screen.

When you have lots of detailed RFP questions, you drastically reduce the chance that evaluators, especially lawyers, will read all of them. It's a simple case of mathematics, especially when lawyers are "voluntold" that they are on the panel convergence project. You also increase the chance that the questions will be too vague, confusing, and even inapplicable.

In other words, they might make things cloudier rather than clearer than you would with a simple and direct approach. If you don't feel comfortable with your RFP questions on innovation or whether they are working for you, you might want to get an outside second opinion. Similarly, a firm competing for a panel spot might consider the innovative approach of providing the answers to the four questions in the preceding paragraph as an executive summary or infographic.

A second factor in the RFP process is sending the RFP to the right firms and obtaining a large enough sample, especially when the lawyers involved in the process will be advocating for few proposals to evaluate. If innovation is a goal, you could do much worse than starting with the firms on Dan Linna's Law Firm Innovation Index (https://www.legaltechlever.com/). Look to firms presenting at innovation conferences, firms who have Chief Innovation Officers (https://biglawbusiness.com/new-breed-of-law-firm-execs-drive-innovation-to-next-level), or other indicators of commitment to legal innovation.

RFP and Pitch Evaluations

I see RFP evaluation as a screening process to determine who gets to make a pitch, much like resume evaluation determines who gets an interview. The actual pitch is what gives you the information you need to make a decision.

The process can go very wrong in both places.

The biggest danger at both points is simply taking outside firms at their word. I have no doubt that every single law firm will tell you not only that they are great at innovation, but their future plans on innovation are amazing. Your task is to cut through the fog and obtain data and evidence that you can evaluate and use to make good decisions, or, at the very least, "good enough for now" decisions.

Another danger is trying to make a final decision on the basis of the response to the RFP. RFP responses should only be used to screen for firms you want to make a pitch, which means, firms you want to hear more details from. That is the job you are doing at the RFP evaluation stage.

In RFP evaluations, you might want to get an outside opinion to help you make the screen on innovation. The odds of any evaluator reading the innovation section in each of 50 several-hundred-page RFP responses are not good. That's not a criticism—it's a recognition of reality.

If innovation is a goal of your panel convergence effort, you will want not just examples, but you will want to meet the innovation team. It is reasonable and prudent to request that the firm's Chief Innovation Officer or head of innovation take 10—15 minutes of a pitch presentation. Again, depending on your comfort level, this might be a place where you want to get an outside second opinion. You will ultimately make the final decision, but sometimes it's good to have someone interpret and validate what you are hearing.

And, lest you forget, you will only get the innovation and technology proposals you ask for.

Follow-up and Maintenance

The panel is announced with great fanfare. Committee members are congratulated and get awards and bonuses. Victory is declared and the convergence team disbands.

Wrong! This is when the real work to make the effort a success begins.

There are many best practices you can find: single points of contact, initial meeting of panel firms, annual summits, introduction of outside counsel management systems, standardizing, and streamlining processes, engagement letters, discounts or flat fee implementation, and the like.

What about in the area of innovation?

Not so much, at this point. And that's why the panel convergence approach can damage or destroy innovation. It's the follow-up and maintenance that matter.

Let me use a bit of a gardening analogy to describe my approach to implementing successful convergence efforts. First, we need the gardeners : people who are responsible on an ongoing basis for the work and the results. We need to prepare the soil to give the project the best start and continuing growth. We need to plant enough seeds (definitely more than we think we need) to improve the chances of harvest. Watering and nourishing, of course. Eliminating weeds and pests. Pruning to focus and enhance our results. Knowing what to harvest and what to throw away. And preparing for the next season. You get the idea. I'm confident that you don't need me to explain the metaphors.

It's hard work that requires constant attention. It's easy to see how these programs can actually destroy innovation.

Too often, the innovation piece of convergence is vague or afterthought. Innovation can get orphaned, with no person or group tasked with supervising the efforts. Once firms are locked into panels, an "incumbency inertia" can take hold, especially if there is an attitude of being "too busy" with "real legal work." By the way, it's vital to screen that attitude out in the selection process if you can. If there is a standard, it becomes what the other panel firms are doing, which can be a reverse incentive. It's easy for all kinds of incentives to get reversed and misaligned. As time goes on, diversity of ideas and innovation are decreased, because there is a limited universe of firms.

No one would be surprised to find that innovation efforts drop off the cliff after the first year the panel is selected. Concrete and specific plans, follow-up, and roadmaps must be put into place or you will see "drift." Far too often, no evaluations, measures, metrics, key performance indicators, goals, or objectives are put into place. There might even be confusion at the basic level of what the firm charges for innovation work or whether it should be charged for at all. Are there systems for tracking efforts and results or giving feedback? Should you be using a formal counsel evaluation tool like Qualmet (http://www.qualmetlegal.com/)? Is there even an intake or workflow tool for innovation projects? Annual meetings with demos and showcases should be required.

There are two final big problems I want to mention. And they are very big.

The first happens when a law department doesn't ask for the innovation efforts or tech recommendations to be made, even if they were part of the winning pitch. The flip of that, of course, is that the firm doesn't pursue these efforts or take the initiative. And we are back to the gardener analogy and a single point of contact approach.

Second, and most important, there are no consequences for failure to provide the innovation work. Think back, for a moment, to the earlier story about a firm that had not changed a panel in fifteen years. What possible incentive could there be for those panel firms to change or take initiatives? In my legal career, the biggest surprise has been the unwillingness for corporate clients to fire outside firms that are not producing as promised. In this area, I'd be tempted to give the outside firms, as a first innovation project, designing a project workflow system with metrics, standards, and agreed-upon consequences built into it. And then I would challenge you to hold them to it.

Simply put, if you cannot weed out firms that aren't delivering, you really don't have much of a chance of overall success. Your panel convergence process will become a place where innovation goes to die. It's a buyers' market out there and there are alternatives, including alternative legal service providers.

Innovation Driver

Here's my radical, but probably not surprising, proposition: properly done, panel convergence can drive your innovation efforts forward, align business goals, enhance collaboration, and achieve innovation wins and meaningful "return on innovation" with measurable value.

There's a technique in design thinking referred to as "reversal" or "inversion." What happens if we flip over our assumptions, change the end user, look through the opposite end of the telescope, and, well, you get the idea.

In simplest terms, if you reverse any of the points in the previous section, you start to move down the path to drive innovation efforts forward. Try it out as a thought experiment. I'll still be here when you get back.

Oh, wait. I do have an even more radical idea. Outside firms should consider providing innovation services for free and part of their offering to be on the panel.

Here are twelve ways that you might consider using your panel convergence project to drive innovation from your panel firms.

1. Use the panel to make it easy for outside firms learning the company's business, business goals, and how the law department fits into the business. Encourage them to get an understanding of key problems, constraints, budgets, and objectives. The best innovation will be customer-centered innovation. Everything starts here. How will you make that happen?

2. Make outside counsel put some skin in the game. Jeff Carr's ACES approach of putting part of agreed-upon fees at risk if business results and value are not achieved is one example, but how might you incentivize the behaviors you want? It might be as simple as putting firms into red, yellow, or green status on innovation, with penalties for lack of effort or staying in the red or yellow category.

3. General counsel want to move to new technologies, but typically don't have the resources to investigate and make those decisions. They want their outside firms to share how made their own technology decisions, their experiences, and their recommendations. There are benefits to having firms and clients on the same platforms, especially on collaboration tools. This "want" is often expressed on the in-house side, but rarely acted on by outside counsel.

4. Start with staffing and workflow innovations, with an eye on cost savings, efficiencies, and "right sourcing" (getting the work into the hands of the right person at the right skill level and price). Legal departments are concerned about paying huge hourly rates for "commodity" work. Would using a litigation support project platform like ClariLegal, of which I am on the advisory board, generate cost savings and free up lawyer time?

5. Tracking and monitoring projects should be another priority. Helping address those problem areas will achieve real-world benefits and open doors to future innovation projects. Build on small, measurable successes.

6. Prune the panel list. You cannot freeze the panel for fifteen years. There should be an easy process for adding and dropping panel firms to reflect goals (e.g. diversity), movement (e.g., key lawyer or group moves to new firm), change (law firm mergers), business strategy (move into new markets or product lines), and the like. It is not a great place for an in-house counsel to be when they have to use old-line panel firms to handle blockchain or other new technology issues. A regular in-depth review should also be scheduled with promises tracked and consequences exacted. There is a huge benefit to firms to stay on a panel list and many firms, especially mid-market firms, would be happy to make better offers and better efforts than the incumbent panel firms.

7. Measurement and metrics. Innovation is not some airy, vague set of new ideas. Innovation should produce practical results. With a panel, you can collaborate with firms to agree on appropriate metrics and how to track them.

8. Shared goals and objectives. Aligning the law department's goals and objectives to innovation efforts is a powerful way to set direction and strategy. If the law department knows the business problems its business owners want to solve, and the outside law firms are aligned to solving those problems, the results can be very good for everyone. Innovation should be focused

like a laser on the client's problems. Innovation is fundamentally a client-centered exercise. If the word "value" is not at the top of your discussion list with outside firms, you should be asking yourself why it isn't.

9. Connect the people. I like the idea of having "single points or contact" for innovation efforts, with each firm. Consider at least monthly calls, quarterly design thinking or brainstorming events, and annual "summits" where all of the innovation contacts meet and share ideas and goals.

10. Thoughtfully implement standard innovation practices that fit your culture: proof of concept and other experiments; design sprints and minimum viable product approaches; a portfolio of approaches; collecting stories to share; identifying the right talent; and building on successes. In certain cases, does a firm or law department want to start its own innovation lab or outsource the use of an innovation lab or design group? What outside help do you need and what work should stay as part of your core competence?

11. As part of the effort, put into place a system of communication, collaboration, and incentives. What happens if we turn a great idea into a product? How do we make this organic and self-sustaining? How do we measure early-stage benefits?

12. Focus on the "Why?" first. As I've said, a common principle in innovation is answer the "Why?" first, then move to "What?" and, only then move to the "How?" I don't mention specific technologies much in this chapter, because it will be part of the "how." Your focus should be on first things first.

Isn't all of this way more exciting than getting a 15% discount on standard hourly rates?

Practical Action Steps

I want to end this chapter with a bunch of practical action steps. Here are some for you to consider:

1. Make a firm decision that you want to want to use panel convergence to drive innovation in legal services. Start with the "Why?" If you get that question answered, your path becomes so much easier to see.

2. Review your panel convergence RFP, especially on innovation and technology, and simplify, simplify, simplify. What do you want to know that matters? Ask only that.

3. Require an outside firm's Chief Innovation Officer or innovation team to present as part of the pitch presentation. That is who you will be working with on actual projects.

4. Develop a framework and approach to evaluating RFP responses and pitches. Obtain good data and evidence.

5. Request (or volunteer) to participate in design sprints, innovation labs, or productization efforts with panel firms. Offer your problems and issues as experiments for the firm to work on. There's no harm in asking if participation comes with no charge. Firms need plenty of client feedback on their own efforts.

6. Find ways to get outside firms to put skin in the game. Be creative and see what else is happening in the industry, and in other professions.

7. Measure activity and create a simple set of metrics and key performance indicators to track. Then act upon them and track your results.

8. Be constantly on the lookout for internal resources who would be happy to participate in innovation efforts. Results will be mixed, at best, if you assign unwilling lawyers to participate.

9. See innovation as a process of experimentation and learning. Some things will work and some will not. You can learn from both results.

10. When in doubt, give people logoed T-shirts. We are all humans, after all.

For outside firms, or those who want to be on panels, use the reversal or inversion method on the practical action steps above and you'll see your own list.

I've become intrigued how an often-clunky existing process with mixed results—panel convergence—can, if properly handled, be turned into an engine to drive innovation. Having vision is important, as is being willing to make hard decisions and do experiments. ***Panel incumbency should not mean entitlement and tenure.*** There are many firms, with mid-market firms being especially interesting because of motivation and nimbleness, who are able and willing to step up on innovation efforts to provide measurable value for key clients. Lack of action has consequences. The legal market says that it is ready to innovate. Let's see firms and law departments prove it.

 PRO TIP: Outside law firm panel convergence efforts, if properly understood, provide some of the best opportunities for innovation success.

43

Key Client Programs

———————

L aw firms focused on client engagement often establish key client programs for their most important clients. These programs offer special benefits for those clients and are designed to increase retention and new business from those clients. With these programs, a firm can better understand a client's business, risk tolerance, and policies and procedures, align with key client business goals and future plans, and engage with and have better access to decision-makers. In a sense, the key client program offers some the same advantages, although in a more limited way, of bringing legal work in house.

Similarly, many corporate procurement departments have key supplier programs. In these programs, a small number (perhaps ten or so) of suppliers are identified as key suppliers based on amount of spend, business importance, and the like. The company then invites these key suppliers to get more closely aligned with the business, have access to strategies and roadmaps, and offer input into decisions. In turn, the suppliers might adjust their own road-maps and make changes to help the customer.

Outside law firm panels are one form of a key supplier program.

Adding access to your innovation program as a benefit to your key client program is an approach that has great potential, if done well. If you drop the ball, it could be disastrous. First, you bring additional client value without being asked to do so. Second, you have an opportunity to work with clients on their specific problems. Third, you differentiate yourself as an innovation doer, not just an innovation talker. Fourth, you make it harder for another competitor firm to displace you. There are other reasons that I'm sure you can add.

Similarly, a corporate law department might require panel firms to provide innovation programs as part of the RFP or as a requirement for staying on the panel, as discussed in Chapter 43. Metrics and follow-up will be important if you take this approach.

If you and your innovation program become part of the offering of a key client program, the business development team becomes your ally, helps you get access to the firm's best clients, and, perhaps most important, opens up access to the business development group's budget.

As far as pricing of innovation efforts as part of a key client program, I know that I'm a radical because I believe they should be free to your client. They can be seen as a deal sweetener in panel RFPs. By free, I mean that, as in-house counsel, I do not want to pay my outside law firms for my participation in creation, prototyping, and initial product development. I would, however, expect to pay, with an early adopter discount, for what is developed once it becomes a completed product. I would also consider co-development and other partnering or investing arrangements in the case of productized services. You might recognize a type of freemium business model in this approach.

Best of all, engaging with a key client program allows you to have great testers for new efforts, identify problem areas that exist in other clients, high-quality case studies, and increased visibility for what you have accomplished. Those are a lot of big wins.

 PRO TIP: If you are in a law firm, try to leverage the business development team as your ally in finding innovation partners. If you are in a corporate law department, try to leverage the panel RFP process to find innovation partners.

44

Collaborating with Other Firms

Y ou might be thinking, "Yes, the ideas in this chapter are great for large organizations, but I'm in a medium-sized or small organization. What might work for me?"

Hmmm, it might be time for you to do a little brainstorming on that.

Here's an idea to get you started. What if you collaborate with a group of similar organizations to get more contributions and split the costs?

You might look to other local for regional firms or law departments, other organizations with the same specialty areas, or even look to local law schools or alumni groups or bar associations as the container for group efforts. Many firms today are part of national or global networks, like Lex Mundi or The Network of Trial Law Firms, or malpractice carriers like ALAS or LawPro (in Canada).

One potentially fertile approach would be a local business community approach, where you brought in law firms, law departments, the law school(s), and business leaders for an event. Targeting the local startup community is an obvious opportunity to consider.

Think about the value of constraints. Is not being big enough a wall too high to climb or does it point you to different doors? Constraints often lead to new opportunities, if you change your perspective.

 PRO TIP: Look for others that you might collaborate with to increase your reach and reduce your costs.

45

TechPrompts Example

I want to end with an example of an award-winning innovation effort I helped start, how it evolved, and how I will be changing the model going forward into something else. It will illustrate several important aspects of innovation efforts.

As with all good innovation projects, it begins with a conversation with a customer.

Since I first became an information technology lawyer (and probably even earlier than that), I've been in meetings with clients and other lawyers where I started to get scared that the clients were going to hug me because I actually understood their technology and its potential and implications. Many lawyers simply do not realize how frustrating it is for tech-savvy clients to deal with lawyers who don't understand technology and seem to be unwilling to make any effort to educate themselves. You can bring increased value to a client by being up to speed on technology, their business, and the ecosystem they are part of. That's not, as they say, rocket science. But it is both a real and a perceived problem for many clients. Just ask them.

Without going into any specifics, I started to represent/cover a business unit that was moving forward very quickly with a new technology. For our purposes, let me say that it was APIs (application programming interfaces).

On my first call with the group leader, I was asked in the exasperated tone that technology people can take with lawyers who they don't think know anything at all about technology, "Do you even know anything about APIs?"

I said, "I don't claim to be an expert, but here's what I do know." I knew what API stood for and meant, what APIs do, why they are important, how excited I was about their potential, what I had done to educate myself, and how I actually used some APIs, including one that posted my tweets automatically as Facebook updates. I explained that what I didn't know was how to look at the details of the coding of an API or to create one of my own. That took me about a minute, because I had prepped, had notes, and was excited to be involved in this work.

There was a long pause.

He said, "You know a lot. And I can teach you the technical stuff if you want, but all you really need to do is go play with the APIs we have created and you'll pick it up quickly."

As a result, I was able to quickly achieve everything that lawyers like to have with clients: early involvement in projects, clients asking questions rather than avoiding talking to the lawyer, and being invited to group meetings as a participating member. The tangible proof: I got a package one day shortly after the call with a T-shirt, a jacket, and the group's hoodie.

I thought about whether any interested lawyer could be prepped for a meeting that involved technology with a one-pager that gave a plain language definition of the technology with examples, listed the main legal issues involved with the use of the technology, and set out a list of simple questions that would move the process forward. For example, if the topic of the meeting was cloud computing, a question about whether it involves a private, public, or hybrid cloud or even the physical location of the servers would demonstrate some level of knowledge and engagement, and help get necessary information to use in the legal portion of the project.

I ran the idea by a few of my colleagues for a sanity check, and then pitched the idea to some of my business owners. They really liked the idea, so I decided to flesh it out with a very small group.

The first iteration was a list of twelve or so technology topics (blockchain, APIs, cloud computing, et al.), the one-pager framework as a prototype, and a small intranet site that had the one-pager, a list of useful resources, and links to people with expertise and familiarity with the topic. You'll recognize both the mini-knowledge management portal and expert locator concepts in this pitch.

After more feedback and more pitches, the basic plan was approved for three initial topics, with the addition of an attempt to get people who wanted to volunteer to help or learn involved in the process (rather than have a small core team of content producers). The request for volunteers got much more response than we expected. The notion of building a learning community and webinars got added to the plan. And, once lawyers got involved, lawyers preferred an extensive white paper to a one-pager. Not a big surprise for those who work with lawyers.

The additional features made the initial effort much harder than just going with an MVP based on the original prototype, but the project was successful enough to win an award.

There are plenty of lessons in this example. You will probably even see some that I haven't. You will see the role of a story, a problem, and pains and gains analysis, involving customers (here, there were several different customer categories) in the process and getting feedback, and an experimentation and iteration loop. In the second round of topics, we incorporated learnings from the first round.

While I liked the evolution of this project, I keep going back to the core idea before it got more complicated: the one-pager that a lawyer can grab and read before or even during a meeting, with pointers for resources, and expert location. I'm working on a variation of this as a product I'm calling TechPrompts. You'll hear more from me about that in the future. If you would be interested in providing feedback on that concept, please reach out to me.

 PRO TIP: Take time to look at other innovation projects and see what you learn from them.

PART VI

RISK AND PORTFOLIO MANAGEMENT

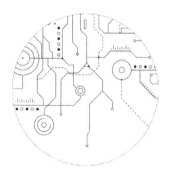

46

Evaluating, Auditing, and Internal Reporting

---

t's tempting to spend much of your time in the "fun" parts of innovation and concentrate on "creative work." I'm the same way. However, you also need to assess, evaluate, and even audit your results on a regular basis. Then, you need to report those findings to the management of the organization and other stakeholders. The skills you learn doing these things will translate directly to what you will want to evaluate and report to customers. So, let's roll up our sleeves and see what you need to do.

First, I recommend that you resist the urge to delegate all of this to a subordinate. Your familiarity with these numbers, how they are obtained, and being able to explain what they mean going forward will be a key part of keeping your job and getting the support you need to move your efforts forward. Showing that you have good, clear-headed grasp of actual, relevant results and what they mean will help you establish trust and confidence of decision-makers quickly.

That doesn't mean that you have to collect and organize all the data into a spreadsheet yourself. However, you do need to know how that data was collected and what the spreadsheets show. If you lead an innovation team, your role should be more one of data reporting design than spreadsheet data entry.

Look at evaluation efforts from four perspectives: what you want/need to know; what your team wants/needs to know; what your management wants/needs to know; and what you customers or collaborators want/need to know. You will want to get in a readily-digestible for, not only what you want, but everything in the three other categories.

The information each of us wants will vary, so a big part of the evaluation effort is determining what's most important to you. If you aren't sure, pick some to start with and experiment with them. Chapter 36 on key performance indicators will give you some good ideas. For the other categories, you will want to ask want people want to see and how often. In addition, you will want to take the initiative and suggest other reporting data for those other groups to consider that you think would be important to show insight and initiative.

Although I recognize that this suggestion might be difficult to implement and might seem like overkill for a small team, carefully consider creating a real-time reporting tool that pulls automatically from other data-capture tools from the beginning of your effort. It's easier to have extra capacity that you can grow into rather than trying to put in a new reporting tool on the fly later.

Use a dashboard approach, whether it's separate "cover" spreadsheet that automatically pulls numbers from underlying spreadsheets into a one-page format that you like or a separate dashboard that pulls data from other enterprise tools.

My simple test for a dashboard is to imagine who might call me and what information they might be asking me for on that call. My dashboard should place the answers to those questions at my fingertips. If someone asks me a question I can't answer, I'm likely to add it to my dashboard. Trust me, you'll like seeing adjectives like "well-organized," "responsive," and "prepared" on your annual evaluation.

While I encourage you to design what you need for evaluation for yourself, it's definitely a place where you can get assistance or even a "second pair of eyes" to check what you are doing.

If you don't have an evaluation system in place, you are likely to get into the world of audit. In fact, if you inherit an innovation program that does not have a good evaluation and reporting system in place, you are likely to have an audit of what is going on as your first priority. An independent or outside "audit" can also be helpful when you feel that your closeness or involvement in a project you love has impinged on your objectivity or even if you have only a vague sense that a project has gone off the rails.

Warning signs that you might be approaching a closer evaluation of audit stage include:

1. Continuing delays with vague explanations

2. Budget overruns

3. Projects staying in the "98% done" stage

4. Continuing problems with technology or tools

5. Customer frustration or objections to the offering

6. Technological compatibility issues or bugs

7. Choice of non-standard tech platform creating other problems

8. A great idea for offering is getting no traction in market

9. Overloading certain employees and underloading others

10. People not busy enough or far too busy

11. Discovering that customers either have a similar tool they are already using or might be interested in your offering if it did something else instead

12. Just to name a few: there is plenty of literature on signs that a project is in trouble

There will come a point when you will have to step up to this problem, and the sooner the better. Evaluation systems, regular team meetings, and similar efforts will help address these issues earlier in the process, but it's surprisingly easy to get to a point where you need some help.

That help might come in the form of a "sanity check" or second opinion that you are on the right track. It might be something that looks at your efforts in the larger context of what is happening in the market. It might be a deep dive into what is really going on. In other words, you might need a true audit to locate and identify problems that are derailing your efforts. As an example, I often talk with people who I see are working on projects when there are already plenty of commercial solutions for the same problems.

Finally, reporting. Taking ownership of reporting and setting the framework, format and cadence of report show that you understand business needs, are willing and able to set the terms of the discussion, and are a communicative team player who takes initiative. Lots of good words to see in your annual evaluation. It also helps you get an understanding and agreement on how success is determined, what metrics are important, and what reporting is expected and required. Getting those agreements avoids miscommunication.

Although internal reports don't always get read, the fact that they exist is important to decision-makers. If you have agreed to deadlines and requirements for reporting, you must meet them, no matter what else you think has priority. Even an email on a report's due date saying that it will be delayed for X reason is far preferable to missing a reporting deadline and being asked where the report is.

Reporting is a place where innovation leaders distinguish themselves. And, as I mentioned, the reporting techniques and skills you develop transfer will to great customer service and communication.

 PRO TIP: If someone in management called you right now, what numbers and data would you like to have at your fingertips to answer questions on the spot. Build a simple reporting dashboard to give you that.

47

Risk Alignment: Portfolios and Portfolio Management

———————

The external approach that has probably had the most impact on my legal career has been modern portfolio theory, which won a Noble Prize for economist Harry Markowitz in 1990. You will be familiar with a primary concept of it—diversification of risk—in connection with financial investments, but principles of the approach have been applied in many different contexts.

Early in my career, I practiced in the area of estate planning. The Uniform Prudent Investor Act allowed for a modern portfolio approach to be taken by fiduciaries under the definition of "prudence," along with evaluation of the entire portfolio as a whole rather than a second-guessing of the performance of each individual asset in isolation.

There are a few key points to keep in mind. First, that diversification across risk categories, including high-risk categories, is the least-risky approach. Second, emphasizing only the "safest" investments is likely, over time, to be the least safe approach. Think about being invested only in AAA safe bonds when a period of high inflation happens. Third, factors like timeframe, risk-tolerance, and the like play an essential role in portfolio creation and maintenance.

Today, "target year" investments (mutual funds and ETFs) can be purchased that have stock and bond allocations that adjust as you just closer to retirement or another goal. Finally, for our purposes, it's the whole portfolio and its alignment with our goals that becomes the focus.

Too often, especially in the case of lawyers, the goal becomes risk management, which actually is risk avoidance. In the realm of innovation, that approach can be difficult because of the lack of certainty about the likely success of innovation efforts and, as in the case of business startups, the high likelihood of failure.

That must be balanced against both the potential risk of staying the same and the extraordinarily high returns of some innovation projects. If you take a portfolio approach, you can navigate these waters much more easily than if you evaluate each project in isolation with an emphasis only on risk avoidance.

In addition, in an interesting aspect of many human psyches, we care more about loss-avoidance than gain-achievement. Studies show that it upsets most of us more to have a loss than to have a gain. That leads to resistance to change and plays a big role in how many people approach innovation efforts and change.

There are two areas I want to highlight: (1) risk personality identification and risk tolerance, and (2) portfolio construction and evaluation. I'll wrap up with a look at how those two areas intertwine.

Risk Personalities and Risk Tolerance

If you read even a little about financial investments, you'll see investors classified into categories like low risk, medium risk, and high risk, or cautious, moderate, and aggressive. Investments are described in similar ways.

You can even take any number of quizzes and tests to determine what type of investor you are. In more sophisticated testing, timeframe, age, goals, and the like might be factored in to be a bit more precise about where you sit on the risk personality continuum. Note that your risk personality might change over time.

Once you have a good idea of your risk personality, you can start to assemble investments that best fit your risk personality. I call this risk alignment and it applies to organizations and teams as well as individuals. Aligning your investments with your risk personality becomes an important goal and strategy, whether in the financial realm or the innovation realm.

The problem that arises if we look at risk personality and risk alignment in isolation is that we are likely to simply match personality type and investment. For example, there would be a tendency to pick only moderate investments if you have a moderate risk personality. Under portfolio theory, that would be a mistake.

Portfolio Construction and Evaluation

When we construct a portfolio, we are making decisions about our invest goals, our risk profile, timeframes, and the like, all with the context of diversification. The word "prudence" is quite appropriate here.

We understand that the highest level of risk, over time, comes from the non-diversified portfolio. As a result, we should construct and maintain a portfolio that is a mix of low-risk, medium-risk, and high-risk assets, with diversity across asset classes, all in alignment with our investment goals and risk personality.

Whether you use traditional financial descriptions, as I have in this chapter, innovation models, business models, or other approaches, your goal is to create a diversified, mixed portfolio. Over time, you manage the portfolio by rebalancing the mix of the components to so it accurately reflects your desired portfolio, until you reassess and change your portfolio assumptions.

Combining the Approaches

I suspect that you already see where I am going. If you can assess and define the risk personality and risk tolerance of your organization, you can establish a context and framework into which you can fit your innovation efforts and your innovation portfolio that will feel comfortable to you and your organization. Then you can design your portfolio so that it reflects accurately that personality and tolerance. It's a simple and powerful approach.

There are three aspects of this approach that appeal to me.

First, it is simple, easy to understand, and matches how most of us think about investing these days.

Second, it lends itself to visual representations. You can make a chart that shows the different risk/return categories and map your projects. It will then be easier to see if efforts are concentrated in one area and completely missing from others. The makes it easier to have discussions about taking on some riskier efforts.

Third, there is a possibility of scoring the different parts of this approach and using math to get a bit more precision. For example, if your organization has a risk tolerance score of (I'm making this up) 33 and a risk/return score of 15 in its existing innovation efforts, you could argue that it's actually prudent to add a project with a risk/return score of 75 (or 50 or anything over 33) to your portfolio and your organization would still be comfortably within its risk tolerance range. I see other potential uses and insights to be gained by analyzing efforts on a portfolio basis.

A final thought: The term "moonshot" is sometimes used for super-high-risk, super-high-potential projects. Using an innovation portfolio approach, you can create some space for a "moonshot" as part of an overall prudent approach.

I'm planning, after finishing this book, to put some effort into creating this kind of a portfolio assessment/alignment tool. If this interests you and you might be interested in piloting, please contact me.

 PRO TIP: A portfolio approach turns innovation efforts into types of investments and offers ways to manage investments in the same way you manage your retirement plans and other investments.

48

Increasing and Decreasing Investment

Good practice requires that you have several (or many) innovation projects in flight at the same time, especially when you launch your innovation program. In many case, an equal amount is invested in each program, meaning that they all have the same budget. How do you make decisions about investments and budgets going forward?

Treating every project equally does not make sense, especially in the long term. You want to identify likely winners and likely losers, introduce new projects into the mix, and respond to customer input and feedback. In a real sense, you need to prune your project portfolio on a regular basis.

If we accept that at least 90% of efforts are going to fail (or, in the best-case scenario, pivot to something completely different), it's important to get out of the efforts likely to fail early and keep concentrating on those likely to succeed. That's easier said than done, for a variety of reasons, not the least of which are our psychological attachment to our favorite ideas and the sunk-cost fallacy.

A method of handling investment and budget that I like is to evaluate efforts on a regular, short basis (e.g., quarterly) and ruthlessly cut budgets or eliminate projects not going anywhere and move their funding to projects that are working by using measures you decide upon in advance.

As an aside, budget is often less important for innovation efforts than people believe. If you cut the budget on a project and people continue to work on it or potential customers are still interested in it, you might have identified a winning project that you might increase the budget for later. The timing might just be wrong.

You might establish a cadence where at the end of each quarter, you look at the current projects and future projects and, in an unsentimental, clear-eyed way (and I KNOW this is hard), assess their success and potential. Then you make some decisions. Will a new effort replace a current struggling effort? Are there winners that need more investment? Are there projects that haven't taken off that are not likely to succeed in a reasonable time? Is it already clear that you've missed the mark with an effort?

There are a number of ways to assess "winners" and the criteria I would use are likely to be somewhat different than what you might use. For example, if there is a project, no matter what I think of it personally, that has already gotten the commitment of a customer for a pilot, it goes into my winner category. With customer commitment, I know that I can argue for additional funding if needed, especially if I've established that agreement with management from the beginning.

By the way, if a customer is willing to pay for a pilot or provide funding for the effort, it's definitely a winner.

As for the efforts that don't make the cut, well, that is not an easy task, especially if you feel a personal attachment to or investment in the project or the team working on it. Avoid calling those projects "losers." If you are setting up a culture where failure is applauded, you might call them failures, but if you don't yet have that culture, I'd avoid that as well.

Have the conversation, discuss the evidence and data, debate the options, decide and move on. As I mentioned, in some cases, you might find that people committed on some projects might continue to work on them in their spare time and argue later why they are good projects. I would not discourage that, other than to say their assigned projects come first, they must on the on their own time, and everyone agrees that the project has no guarantee of ever being reinstated.

Be sure to take the time and effort to have after-assessment meetings about projects that don't go forward to capture lessons learned and to determine if there are parts of those projects that can be used in other projects. Keep the focus on the experimental and learning sides of innovation.

Another aspect of investment decisions is the simple, but often profound, choice of whether to buy or build. Fortunately, Melissa Perri's book, *Escaping the Build Trap: How Effective Product Management Creates Real Value*, is a great resource on that issue.

What if this approach just seems too hard? Here's when using an external advisor can help. Your innovation committee, advisory board, or an outside consultant can help you make the most difficult decisions because they will be more objective than you are likely to be, especially if you have a close-knit team.

PRO TIP: Make budget and investment allocations a key result arising out of your project evaluations to increase the risk of finding winners and pruning projects not likely to succeed in the short-term.

49

Changing Course and Pivoting

Sometimes you start out with great idea, have a bunch of internal discussions and convince yourself that the idea is even better, and then it crashes and burns on first contact with customers and the outside world. You realize that you have been going in the wrong direction. What do you do?

In Eric Ries's book, *Lean Startup*, he describes the notion of pivoting. Many successful companies have in their histories a huge change in course after a near-failure. There are many examples. Intel pivoted from memory chips to microprocessor chips. Google pivoted from being a search engine to an advertising-placement company.

One of the best examples is Twitter. Twitter started as a podcasting service called Odeo. One day, Apple announced that it would make podcast distribution available through iTunes. Odeo saw that there was no future in its podcasting business. They looked at what else they had and identified a personal updates platform they used internally called Twitter. They pivoted to that business and, as they say, the rest is history, although you can certainly argue that the history of Twitter has several other major pivots.

Not all pivots are successful as the Twitter pivot. However, innovation efforts are like startup companies and similar principles apply.

Once you get prototypes and MVPs into the hands of customers and testers and get feedback, course changes are likely. This is especially true if you did not have much customer involvement in the early parts of the design process.

What is the best way to handle this? Accept that it is likely to happen. Adopt an experimentation and learning mindset. Listen carefully to what your customers say and, just as important, to what they are not saying. Ask your customers to tell you what they think your product is and what it does, and see how that tracks with what you think they should be saying. Even better, with cloud tools, you might be able to get analytics that tell you what users are actually doing rather than only what they tell you they think that they are doing.

Course changes and pivots can often happen where you unknowingly re-created something that already exists in the market, especially if customers are familiar with the other product. You can move away from that product or determine how it (or certain parts of it) do a job that the existing product does not get done in another way.

You might also have to pivot when you brilliantly create a product or services that no one wants or that people would love if it were free to them or unprofitable for you.

Course changes are also part of the scientific method and other innovation processes. Keep your eyes, ears, and mind open and be ready to adjust when necessary, and, sometimes, in big ways.

 PRO TIP: You might not ever have to do a full-blown pivot, but you will definitely be making course changes. Become familiar with concept and open to making needed changes.

PART VII

HANDLING A FEW HARD THINGS

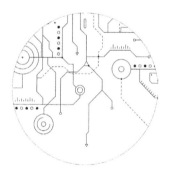

50

Unexpectedly Hard Stuff

———————

There's a great book about start-up business by Ben Horowitz called *The Hard Thing About Hard Things: Building a Business When There Are No Easy Answers*. It is a handbook about all kinds of things that can go wrong when you start a business. Some are impossibly hard, but Ben worked through them and shares what he did. To give a flavor for the book, imagine launching your product on September 11, 2001. Highly recommended.

He also covers some things you might run into, from needing to fire co-founders and longtime friends, having key people leave just when you need them, and much more. It's both scary and some of the most real advice you could ever get about running a business.

Much of that might apply in your innovation team and efforts. In this chapter, I wanted to mention a few things I've seen that can be unexpectedly hard to deal with.

► **Stepping Away from Your Favorites.** I believe that one of the most important and hard-to-find traits in a chief innovation officer or other innovation leader is being able to step back from your favorite ideas and projects, assess them objectively, and kill your favorites, if necessary. It's very easy to get too involved in one of your original projects and not be able to look at the whole program as you need to do.

- ▶ **Communicating with Lawyers and Other Management.** There are times when you will believe that you are speaking in different languages and need a translator. Lawyers are especially good at seeing problems and putting you on the spot. That's one reason why gathering data and having a dashboard can be a big help.

- ▶ **Delegation is Easier than it Looks.** Many innovators are great at ideas and working on their own. They are hard to manage. If you are in that family of people, managing people and handing off tasks to them can be difficult. Innovation teams are built on trust. Delegating important tasks is one practical way to build an environment of trust. The good news is that you can be taught how to delegate.

- ▶ **Creating a Zone of Safety.** Research at Google indicated that a key present in successful teams is the creation of a zone of safety. People feel that they can speak up without negative consequences. There are techniques that you can use. The zone of safety is a fragile thing and it's easy to destroy.

- ▶ **Turnover.** Remember that creatives value working on cool projects with great people over traditional motivators like titles and even money. They will move on to something better for the chance to work on a cool project or leave to take on a new challenge or just for a change. You need to do what you can on retention, but it's even more important to create onboarding and other systems to bring new people up to speed quickly and to building ongoing relationship with people who leave, because they might well come back for the right project.

- ▶ **The Legal Sales Cycle.** It is difficult for many people to understand how long and convoluted the legal buying cycle can be. Months can go by even when your customer keeps telling you that they are ready to buy. These delays can have many ripple effects and it's one reason why you want to have several efforts going on at once.

- ▶ **The Legal Approval Cycle.** Both your customer and your organization might also have procurement or approval requirements (e.g., extensive RFP requirements and processes) that also can take months. Contract negotiations can also be difficult.

- ▶ **Confidentiality.** The more involved your customer is and the more they share, especially about future plans, the more emphasis they will put on confidentiality. You might need confidentiality as well. However, you also want to reduce friction and the need to negotiate non-disclosure agreements ("NDAs"). You need to get a good understanding of what your customer cares about and, ideally, see if either you can sign their standard NDA or can offer them an NDA that has terms that are standard in the market. Even more important than an NDA, get a solid understanding of the actual processes and procedures that must be used to safeguard confidential information once it is exchanged. Other common approaches are to agree not to exchange confidential information or require clear labels.

- ▶ **Intellectual Property.** I have lived in this world of IP for many years, so I've seen a lot. This area can get complicated. Remember that, as a general principle, ideas alone are not intellectual property in the United States. And, as a general principle, copyright protection automatically attaches to creative works. Even with that said, it can get hazy very quickly, especially when you offer something like design sprint. A full discussion of these issues goes way beyond the scope of this book. A few practical suggestions: take a "what you bring stays your IP, what we bring stays our IP" approach and focus on what happens with something new; push discussion of joint IP down the road until a decision is made to jointly develop a product; clearly carve out your right to use what you create that by its nature is intended and expected to be reusable; clearly establish that you are not transferring IP ownership of your IP you use in other products; get the licenses you need to use anything created; and walk through examples of what you want to be sure you can do and get clarifications and agreement around those uses. You will want to get an IP lawyer involved in this process.

► **Case Studies, Articles, and Mentioning Customers.** One of the best things about pilots is that they make for great case studies, white papers, and press releases. Secure the permission for this early in the process and get your customer engaged in the effort. Do not be surprised if a customer has limitations or must get internal approvals. Also, many consultants like to talk about their customers and what they have done for them. Many customers do not like that at all and there may be contract terms in place to prevent that. Make sure that you are on the same page as your customer on these points. Since the best publicity and marketing results are likely to come from a joint effort between you and your customer, make it easy for your customer to do that.

- ▶ **Politics.** Wait, you thought your job was about innovation. You might spend most of your time dealing with internal politics. I know of many examples where one lawyer stopped a whole project because of a personal agenda. Here's a place an executive sponsor, mentor, or coach might be a big help. However, nothing can prepare you for the byzantine politics of a legal organization.

None of this should be a deterrent or too overwhelming; just expect that there will be some unexpectedly hard stuff that you will need to deal with.

 PRO TIP: Ben Horowitz's book, The Hard Thing About Hard Things: Building a Business When There Are No Easy Answers, is the best resource I know for getting prepared for the unexpectedly hard stuff that will arise.

51

Barriers and Handling Objections

———————

L awyers are trained to think in ways that can be the opposite of good innovation practices. They spot issues and potential problems, with the emphasis on problems. They identify and manage risks, with the emphasis on risks. They focus on process, procedure, and precedent. Saying that something "has always been done this way" is seen as high praise for lawyers. Law has long been characterized as a "conservative" profession.

At the same time, legal work often is creative, innovative, and forward-thinking. At least that's the case on legal matters, but much less so on the actual practice of law, new business models, and big ideas about the practice itself.

As a result, implementation of change, technology, and big, bold, new ideas too often either doesn't happen or happens at a glacial pace. However, the combination of these two aspects of lawyers—conservative practice approaches and creative legal approaches—holds the key to identifying and smashing through barriers to breakthroughs in the practice.

In this chapter, I will map out twelve common barriers to legal innovation. Simply naming and identifying them will help you examine and challenge them. Do they really have to be barriers? Or can they be turned into opportunities? And I'll suggest some ways for you to start overcoming these barriers and move your efforts forward.

Let's see how many of the following barriers are familiar to you.

1. **Too Busy**. How many long conversations have you had with lawyers in which they tell you in painstaking detail how over busy they are and have no time for anything—except, seemingly, to tell you at length how busy they are. Michael Gerber, author of the book, *The E-Myth Attorney*, says that we should spend as much time working on our practices as we do in our practices. The move to massive minimum billable hours requirements has had a corrosive effect on the practice, especially in reducing the amount of time available to rethink and make changes to how lawyers work. Are there really not enough hours in your day?

2. **Legal Exceptionalism.** Many lawyers believe that everything they do is unique and cannot be standardized. Sometimes this belief is summed up by saying that law is a profession, not a business. There is a tendency to see every aspect of legal work as custom and unique. From fussing with fonts and margins on invoices to a wide variety of arcane procedures, many lawyers insist on long-standing personalized approaches appreciated only by them rather than moving to more efficient and standard processes that can be delegated to others. Is everything you do in your practice actually a "legal" process?

3. **No One Else is Doing This**. Lawyers sometimes need to feel the comfort of knowing that they are not the first to try something and that other lawyers are doing the same things, especially in technology. There is an interesting pattern in legal technology where certain software tools become prevalent in certain cities as a result of lawyers talking to each other. The fact that others are doing something helps lawyers get com-

fortable that a change is not too radical. This approach tends to make many lawyers followers, rather than leaders. Are you making sure someone else you know has implemented a new idea before you decide to look into it for yourself?

4. **Someone Else is Doing This, So We Can't.** The interplay of this barrier and the previous one, which sometimes can occur in the same conversation, is fascinating. If a competitor is working on a new approach or technology, some lawyers will say that they don't want to copy. They might also say that if X is doing it, it must be a bad idea because X isn't so smart. This reaction might not be a bad thing if it pushes you to act and explore different options but it, too often, it shuts down the change process. Is the "not invented here" mindset slowing you down?

5. **Not Asking the Client.** Clients, especially corporate clients, are on record as saying that they want their lawyers to bring them new ideas and innovations. Truth be told, many lawyers do not like to have direct conversations about their work with their clients. Many lawyers hate to send bills, let alone suggest new approached and changes to the existing relationship. The key to innovation is getting the client involved and solving the client's real problems, not assuming that you know what the client wants. On at least an annual basis, are you sitting down with key clients to talk about improvements to the relationship and work process?

6. **Catastrophizing.** I once had a law partner who asked his estate planning clients about the "atomic bomb dropped on the family reunion" scenario to get them

to focus on the final, final disposition of their estate to contingent beneficiaries. Lawyers are really good at finding worst-case scenarios and playing devil's advocate. It's a key part of risk assessment. When it seeps into looking at innovation, however, it can become a significant barrier, especially if done reflexively and automatically. "If we try this new technology, everything else will break, we won't be able to do any work and we will have no revenue for six months." "If we suggest flat fees on certain matters to a client, they will fire us on the spot." Risks fall within a set of ranges. Are you too often going to the worst-case scenario when considering a big new idea?

7. **Thinking in Isolation, or Compared to What?** There's a famous philosophy problem about whether it's best to push one person into the path of a train to save five people on the track or to save the one person and have the train hit the five people on the track. It often gets raised in the context of self-driving cars—how can the programming of the car resolve this philosophical dilemma? Our attention focuses on the highly-improbable scenario rather than the reality of 40,000 highway deaths a year in the United States. It can be difficult to step back and look at your practice and your systems in a critical way. It is much easier to look at a new system and compare it to a mythical ideal. Context is important in making big idea decisions. If you were to start over, would you implement your existing system or the new one that you are considering?

8. **Discomfort with Standard Innovation Techniques.** I was recently at a continuing legal education seminar and there was a session on improvisation for lawyers.

The room all but emptied before the session began. I've heard lawyers and other legal professionals complain about and dismiss every innovation and design thinking technique in common use elsewhere—from brainstorming to white boards to, particularly vehemently, post-it notes for capturing ideas. It is important to, as they say, think different. Are you refusing to try standard techniques?

9. **Quality Over Quantity.** The statistics vary, but it looks like you can expect 90% of startups and new initiatives to fail. Many other efforts change drastically. Companies often "pivot" to new business models based on customer feedback. Twitter, originally a podcasting company, is one classic example. In brainstorming exercises, the goal is quantity of ideas. You always want to get lots of ideas expressed and captured. Another primary goal is not to criticize ideas as they get generated. Lawyers tend to want to highlight "quality" ideas and experience stress over quantity. Given the 90% failure rate, the odds of identifying "quality" successfully at an early stage are low. There are better frameworks than "quality." Are you uncomfortable with generating lots of ideas before judging their quality?

10. **Moving too Quickly from Why and What to How.** This barrier is similar to the previous one. The evidence indicates that if you can focus on the actual problems of clients, the job they need to get done, and what reduces their pain and increases their gain, the likelihood of great results is enhanced. Lawyers tend to move too quickly to the "how" to accomplish something. Lawyers like processes and procedures. There is great value in remaining patient and the "why" and "what" stages

before moving to the "how" stage. Are you moving to solutions before you fully understand the underlying problem to be solved and what approach addresses that specific problem?

11. **Not Looking at Other Businesses and Professions**. As I've mentioned elsewhere, doctors have done a great job with online portals in ways that benefit both doctors and their patients. There are many innovations happening in professions and businesses similar to law, and also in those not similar to law: online portals, productization of services, use of video, self-service of all sorts, and much more. Sometimes a fresh perspective is required. How often do you look at the changes in your other customer experiences and wonder how you might try them in your practice?

12. **Not Killing Bad Ideas.** There are many reasons not to recommend being in meetings with lawyers. Looking back on my legal career, I recall the many times—in hiring decisions, technology decisions, motions for action, nominations of officers, and more—where it's clear that there are several excellent options and several that aren't at the same level, have no support, and can be dismissed. Far too often, there will be lawyers who want to give the options that don't make sense a thorough discussion so that "we are sure we are right about them." The end result is exactly what you would expect and valuable time that could spent on the best options is wasted. Are you able to move forward and decide on options ruthlessly and without sentimentality?

I suspect that you can add a few items of your own to the list and that you have your own examples from the above categories.

It's quite an obstacle course of barriers. Can you smash through these barriers?

Here are a few recommendations of ways to break through barriers to big ideas.

1. **Surface Your Biases.** We all lapse into several of the biases mentioned in this chapter. We also tend to have a bias toward the status quo and inaction. Identifying and diagnosing your biases will help you move past them. When considering a new idea, use a framework that helps you test your reactions to an idea or proposal against these barriers. Are you analyzing smartly and critically or are you simply falling back on biases and old methods? A simple checklist or grid might be all you need.

2. **Involve Your Clients.** It is so easy to assume that we know what our clients want without talking to them. The best innovations come out of a thorough understanding of client problems. Identify your clients who are likely to be most interested in new approaches and schedule time to talk to at least two or three of them.

3. **Find Some Standard Techniques You Like.** There are lots of standard design and innovation practices. Some you will hate, but some you will like. That's a good thing. The Value Proposition Canvas discussed in more detail in Chapter 35 is a tool I especially like.

4. **Look at What Works Elsewhere.** Start to pay attention to your customer experience in other settings. Your doctor's online portal might be an eye-opener. What frustrates you? What do you like? Can you try something like that in your practice?

5. **Take a Portfolio Approach.** As I discuss in Chapter 48, I'm a big fan of the modern portfolio theory of investment, which says that it is prudent not to invest just in cautious and "safe" investments, but to diversify and spread your investments across asset classes and risk categories, all in accordance with your own risk tolerance. In simplest terms, this approach mean that it is both necessary and wise to mix in some higher-risk, higher-potential-return investments in your portfolio. The same reasoning applies in innovation and change. Are you creating more risk for yourself by playing it too safe? A simple chart mapping out your innovation "investments" and where they fit in terms of risk is a great approach to thinking about innovation as a portfolio.

It's easy to get overwhelmed when hearing about big new ideas, transformation, and "change or die" predictions. Lawyers have a lot of barriers, some psychological and some self-imposed. Often the answers to questions comes in the opposites. How do I work on big ideas and smash through barriers? With small steps, patience, and resilience.

 PRO TIP: Develop a toolbox for dealing with common barriers.

52

Dealing with Failure / Pulling the Plug

---

ailure is often discussed in innovation. People are encouraged to "fail fast" and to celebrate failure. Some organizations even give awards for efforts on failed projects.

That works in certain cultures. In other cultures, failure is treated as, well, failure, and it can have negative consequences. It's easy to send mixed messages.

It is important to think of failure as part of the positive concept of resilience. We learn and grow from failures. The possibility of failure is part of the scientific method.

Going through a failure situation, however, is difficult. I'm not sure that I've ever met anyone who enjoyed being in a failure situation. They appreciate the learning that came out afterward, but that might come many years later.

Failures might involve not only the termination of a project but also termination of employment (yours or members of your team), relationships, and in a real sense, dreams. There is disappointment and there are difficult choices. Henry Cloud's book, *Necessary Endings: The Employees, Businesses, and Relationships That All of Us Have to Give Up in Order to Move Forward*, is a good resource.

Although failing is expected, don't be cavalier about it. Make sure you learn from it and handle the people issues well. You can develop a thicker skin over time. It might even feel like it gets easier with experience. But failure will always be a challenge.

 PRO TIP: Don't be cavalier about failure and "fast fails"—understand how to prepare for the real-world impact on you and others.

53

Self-Care

———————

The legal industry is not a world known for emphasizing personal well-being and good physical or mental health practices. Stress and "busyness" are synonymous with the legal profession, as is the emphasis on working gigantic numbers of hours. The statistics on depression and alcoholism are, in a word, shocking. If you have a pressing health issue, you might well hear that you should tough it out, work through it, or even told don't let it affect your work. "Work-life balance" mentions sometimes result in snickers or jokes. Ouch.

Other professions, such as social work, incorporate the notion of self-care into their work. There are ongoing education opportunities, activities, and, in some case, having a personal counselor in place. That is not the case, yet, in law. That's one reason why I suggested that you consider asking for a personal coach as part of your original request when you take on an innovation program.

In larger organizations, you will find employee assistance programs, which can be a great help for you and your team. They might provide counseling referrals, pay for counseling sessions, provide education and other resources, and be a source of help when needed. Make it your job to learn what's available and see what presentations your employee assistance program, HR, or other sources can put on for your team.

You will want to be on the watch for yourself and the people who work with you. Metrics and data can help you identifying potential problem areas and issue. The example you set will speak volumes and set the tone for your program. If you work long hours, your team will. If you take regular vacations, your team will.

You have a lot of work on your plate, but reserve a spot for spending time on self-care for you and your team.

 PRO TIP: Take care of yourself.

PART VIII

ACTION STEPS, TIPS, AND RESOURCES

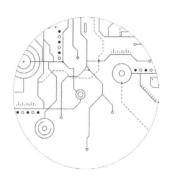

54

Action Steps and Conclusions

A
s I mentioned in the Introduction, creative projects have to reach an end point where they must go off to the market. This book has reached that point. If there are topics that you would like me to add in a future addition, let me know (dmk@ denniskennedy.com). Legal innovation is a conversation. I've set up a LinkedIn group for this book that you can join. It's called Successful Innovation Outcomes in Law and can be found at https://www. linkedin.com/groups/8819641/

I give you permission to highlight, annotate, bookmark, and do whatever else you need to do to absorb what's in this book that appeals to you. It is definitely a book that can be returned to on a regular basis. Some of the tools and approaches will make more sense in certain contexts than they do in others.

It's been a longstanding practice of mine to end all of my presentations with three simple actions steps that you can do after the presentation. I want to end this book in the same way.

None of these should take you more than 15 minutes. None require special tools or technologies, other than a quiet space without interruptions. They are designed to make it difficult for you to come up with excuses not to do them.

1. List three of the visual tools mentioned in this book that you are drawn to. Decide on either (1) a new one that you want to try or (2) one you use but want to get better at. Schedule time on your calendar in each of

the next four weeks to learn more about that tool and experiment with using them.

2. List at least three customers or other stakeholders that you know can and will give you important feedback you need. Invite them to talk with you and schedule the call or meeting in the next two weeks. List the questions you most want to know the answers to.

3. Make three attempts to write new vision or mission statements (one sentence maximum) for your innovation efforts. Let them incubate a day or two, and then see if you can get down to one statement that captures where you want to go.

Legal innovation efforts provide ways for you to experiment and keep learning in the quest to increase customer value and positive change. They also give you the chance to work on cool projects. Count me in and, I hope, you too.

55

Fifty-seven Tips

———————

1. Get to work on innovation, however you define it, and let others talk about definitions while you get the work done.

2. Legal innovation simply means applying innovation techniques in the legal world, in a variety of different dimensions.

3. While focusing only on optimization can have great value, it also narrows your perspective and causes you to miss bigger innovation prizes.

4. Look outside the legal silo and learn the standard types of innovation and business models. Think more in terms of recombining ideas from other sources than creating completely new ideas out of thin air.

5. Understand the fundamental innovation models (and their variants) that already exist and become fluent in the language of these models.

6. Keep the book *Ten Types of Innovation* at the core of your innovation library and, better yet, give it a place of honor on your desk so it's always at hand.

7. Linger in the WHY stage of WHY-WHAT-HOW as long as you can.

8. You MUST get the customer into the conversation at the beginning. Find ways to facilitate those conversations in directed and productive ways.

9. While you will probably gravitate to several favorites, it's a great idea to learn (and maybe even memorize) many of the standard business models to give you a framework and context for your efforts and to help you communicate in the language of business.

10. Diversity is essential in innovation. Take a look around the room at your next meeting. And the one after that. And the one after that.

11. Always emphasize from the beginning that idea generation is about "quantity," but reassure participants, especially lawyers, that they will get to focus on "quality" later.

12. Make a list of the constraints that you believe that you face. Simply writing them down will change your attitude. Then decide whether they are barriers that stop you and why. The others are opportunities to help you move in new directions.

13. What happens if you look at a project and invert the maxim of "people, process, then technology" and frame your effort as "technology, process, then people"? Does it provide a new insight or framework?

14. You must deal aggressively with the "lawyer inhibition factor." A creative idea might be to get a group of lawyers to "brainstorm" a process that optimizes their ideal roles.

15. Not all of the best ideas are contained within your organization. In fact, they rarely, if ever, are. Look outside in thoughtful and strategic ways.

16. Keep your written plan or roadmap simple, keep it short, and keep the reader's attention. Can you get it onto one sheet of paper? Why not?

17. Determine which of the four fundamental innovation categories (mission; targeted but flexible; predetermined product or improvement; "check the box" or "innovation theater") your effort falls into and try to get at least a one-day design thinking or strategic planning event scheduled.

18. If asked to take on an innovation leadership role, make your list of hard questions and get them answered. The fact that you are willing to ask hard, thoughtful questions shows that you are the right person for the role.

19. When hiring personnel and choosing leaders, do not put together a group of people who look and think like you do.

20. Consider looking closely at where you team members are on their career S curves and building for the 15%-70%-15% mix based on placement on the S curve. (See Whitney Johnson's *Building an A Team* for details.)

21. Find yourself a guide or "Yoda" to help you learn how best to sell to your internal audience, enlist and engage your internal champions, and navigate the political landscape.

22. Build some small wins into your project roadmap and use them to build momentum.

23. A well-conceived "show and tell" road trip can kickstart your program and might even generate more projects than you can handle. That's a good thing.

24. Committees are a necessary evil. Don't "have" meetings; lead your meetings. Own your meeting style and set your agendas in advance.

25. It's hard, but you have to be able to ask for help. People often are willing to give you more help than you'd expect. In fact, the help you might ask for might be easier for them to give than what they were afraid you were going to ask them for.

26. Consider the creation of a small advisory board of internal and external experts as part of your pitch for your program or as part of your request for what you will need to take on the program initially or to take it to the next level.

27. If you've ever worked with a coach, you already understand how helpful they can be. Consider building the requirement for coaching for yourself into your job description.

28. "It's just the scientific method" can be a powerful persuader of skeptics.

29. Experiments give us data we can analyze and use for improvement. Stress test your hypotheses. If you don't, your customers will.

30. Find a simple feedback tool and start using it regularly. The old adage is a good one: "Feedback is the breakfast of champions."

31. Develop your own brainstorming style, experiment and see what works best for you and your groups, and

keep people informed about what gets developed out of the session. Ongoing engagement after the session should be a priority goal.

32. Find a form of prototyping that best suits your style and needs and identify who can build those prototypes for you. Remember that a piece of paper can be a prototype.

33. Consider the MVP (Minimum Viable Product) approach when you have a product or service that is "close to done" but has been languishing in the finalization process.

34. Require the completion of a value proposition canvas for any proposed new effort.

35. Take the initiative in recommending KPIs, get agreement from management on those KPIs, and provide regular, one-page, reports on KPI success.

36. Get a decent knowledge of the standard process improvement methods and try to become well-versed in the one that appeals to you.

37. Include space on your team and a line in your budget for at least one project manager.

38. Dream big. Always.

39. Do not cut corners on your own learning. Insist that your employer facilitate your learning and your access to innovation communities and events.

40. Three places to find early wins if you are struggling to find a starting point: simple dashboards, expert locators, and lightweight knowledge management tools.

41. Persuading a general counsel on innovation efforts requires special approaches and language, but these can be learned.

42. Outside law firm panel convergence efforts, if properly understood, provide some of the best opportunities for innovation success.

43. If you are in a law firm, try to leverage the business development team as your ally in finding innovation partners. If you are in a corporate law department, try to leverage the panel RFP process to find innovation partners.

44. Look for others (including other law firms or clients) that you might collaborate with to increase your reach and reduce your costs.

45. Take time to look at other innovation projects, both successful and unsuccessful, internal and external, and see what you learn from them.

46. If someone in management called you right now, what numbers and data would you like to have at your fingertips to answer questions on the spot. Build a simple reporting dashboard to give you that.

47. A portfolio approach treats innovation efforts as types of investments and gives you ways to manage investments in the same way you manage your retirement plans and other investments.

48. Make changes to budget and investment allocations a key result arising out of your project evaluations to increase the risk of finding winners and pruning projects not likely to succeed in the short-term.

49. You might not ever have to do a full-blown pivot, but you will definitely be making course changes. Become familiar with the pivot concept and stay open to making needed changes.

50. Ben Horowitz's book, *The Hard Thing About Hard Things: Building a Business When There Are No Easy Answers*, is the best resource I know for getting prepared for the unexpectedly hard stuff that will arise.

51. Develop a toolbox for dealing with common internal barriers to innovation, progress, and other roadblocks.

52. Don't be cavalier about failure and "fast fails." Understand how to prepare for the real-world and personal impact on you and others. "Resilience" and "learning opportunities" might seem like euphemism, but they can make for a better environment.

53. Take care of yourself.

54. Is there always a reserved seat for your customer at your innovation table?

55. Innovation is a practice and a discipline. Approach your work in that way.

56. If you haven't thought through business model changes as part of your project, you aren't done yet.

57. Keep learning. Every day.

RESOURCES

I f you forced me to pick only three books that I'd recommend that you read as your next steps after finishing this book, I would pick *Ten Types of Innovation*, by Larry Keeley, Ryan Pikkel, Brian Quinn, and Helen Waters, *Value Proposition Design*, by Alex Osterwalder, Yves Pigneur, and Gregory Bernarda, and *The Creative Habit*, by Twyla Tharp. These three books will get you off to a running start.

Books and Other Resources Mentioned in This Book

1. *Creative Strategy: A Guide for Innovation*, William Duggan

2. *Ten Types of Innovation*, Larry Keeley, Ryan Pikkel, Brian Quinn, and Helen Waters.

3. *Value Proposition Design*, Alex Osterwalder, Yves Pigneur, and Gregory Bernarda

4. *Invisible Women: Data Bias in a World Designed for Men,* Caroline Criado Perez

5. *A Beautiful Constraint: How To Transform Your Limitations Into Advantages, and Why It's Everyone's Business*, Adam Morgan and Mark Barden

6. *Disrupt Yourself,* Whitney Johnson

7. *The One Page Business Plan for the Creative Entrepreneur*, Jim Horan

8. *Quiet: The Power of Introverts*, Susan Cain

9. *Building an A Team*, Whitney Johnson

10. *Gridiron Genius*, Mike Lombardi

11. *Lean Startup*, Eric Ries

12. *Business Model Generation*, Alex Osterwalder and Yves Pigneur

13. *Measure What Matters*, John Doerr

14. *The Fifth Discipline: The Art & Practice of The Learning Organization*, Peter Senge

15. *Sprint: How to Solve Big Problems and Test New Ideas in Just Five Days,* by Jake Knapp, John Zeratsky, and Braden Kowitz

16. *Escaping the Build Trap: How Effective Product Management Creates Real Value*, Melissa Perri

17. *The Hard Thing About Hard Things: Building a Business When There Are No Easy Answers*, Ben Horowitz

18. *The E-Myth Attorney*, Michael Gerber

19. *Necessary Endings: The Employees, Businesses, and Relationships That All of Us Have to Give Up in Order to Move Forward*, Henry Cloud

20. Greg Satell's article, "The 4 Types of Innovation and the Problems They Solve" (https://hbr.org/2017/06/the-4-types-of-innovation-and-the-problems-they-solve)

21. https://www.scrum-institute.org/blog/A-Comprehensive-List-of-Business-Models-To-Accelerate-You-and-Your-Business

22. Growth Play—http://www.growthplay.com

23. https://en.wikipedia.org/ wiki/Mind_map

24. Strategyzer—https://www.strategyzer.comn

25. https://www.strategyzer.com/canvas/value-proposition-canvas

26. https://www.strategyzer.com/canvas/business-model-canvas

27. https://legaltalknetwork.com/podcasts/kennedy-mighell-report/2019/02/best-practices-for-measures-and-metrics-in-law-firms/

28. https://www.scoro.com/blog/key-performance-indicators-examples/

29. https://www.thompsonhine.com/uploads/1135/doc/ClosingTheInnovationGapPrint.pdf

30. http://businessoflawblog.com/2016/07/3-business-insights-learned-from-the-dupont-model/

31. https://remakinglawfirms.com/wp-content/uploads/2018/04/Univar-Guidelines-and-Procedures-for-Outside-Counsel.pdf

32. Law Firm Innovation Index—https://www.legaltechlever.com/

33. https://biglawbusiness.com/new-breed-of-law-firm-execs-drive-innovation-to-next-level

34. Qualmet—https://www.qualmetlegal.com

35. ClariLegal—https://www.clarilegal.com

36. FoundationLab—https://www.foundationlab.co

Other Recommended Resources

1. Dennis Kennedy's List of Innovation Resources—https://www.denniskennedy.com/innovation-resources

2. Top 20 Must Read Books on Innovation -https://www.collectivecampus.io/blog/innovation-books

3. https://www.reddit.com/r/Entrepreneur/comments/9s6b1w/top_10_mustread_books_on_innovation/

4. https://www.boardofinnovation.com/staff_picks/100-sources-that-every-innovation-professional-should-know/

5. https://blog.feedspot.com/innovation_blogs/

6. https://www.innovationtraining.org/10-innovation-podcasts-2018/

7. https://www.innovationtraining.org/resources/

8. http://www.legalexecutiveinstitute.com/topics/legal-innovation/

9. https://legaltalknetwork.com/podcasts/law-technology-now/2019/06/innovation-legal-industry-trends-and-opportunities/

10. The Kennedy-Mighell Report podcast

11. A16Z podcast

12. Future Squared podcast

13. https://www.futuresquared.xyz/podcast/episode-270-doblins-ten-types-of-innovation-with-larry-keeley

14. Michigan State University Center for Law, Technology & Innovation (and LegalRnD Lab)—http://www.law.msu.edu/lawtech/index.html

15. Vanderbilt Program on Law and Innovation—https://www.innovatethelaw.com/

16. Stanford Legal Design Lab—https://law.stanford.edu/organizations/pages/legal-design-lab/

17. Ryerson Legal Innovation Zone—http://www.legalinnovationzone.ca/

18. Chicago-Kent's Law Lab—https://www.thelawlab.com/

19. Centre for Legal Innovation (Australia)—https://www.collaw.edu.au/about/centre-for-legal-innovation

20. ABA Center for Innovation—https://www.americanbar.org/groups/centers_commissions/center-for-innovation/

21. ABA Legal Technology Resource Center—https://www.lawtechnology.org

22. Future Law Innovation Programme (Singapore)—https://www.flip.org.sg/

23. *Legal Upheaval: A Guide to Creativity, Collaboration, and Innovation in Law*, Michelle DeStefano

I plan to keep an updated list of innovation resources at https://www.denniskennedy.com/innovation-resources. I'll also share resources on at Successful Innovation Outcomes in Law LinkedIn Group at https://www.linkedin.com/groups/8819641/.

ACKNOWLEDGEMENTS AND INFORMATION

've been fortunate through my life to have many people who encouraged me to try my ideas and create new things. Looking back today, it's surprising to see how many "crazy" ideas I've had have turned into successful and long-running projects and even standard resources and approaches. The biggest learning for me, despite my inclination to want to go it alone, is that innovation is a team sport and you always get the best results when you have the best teams.

There are so many people to thank. First and foremost, Allison Shields freed up a little time from our work on our new LinkedIn book and gave me the opening in my schedule I needed to write this book. My wife, Colleen, and daughter, Grace, supported me in the decision to make the effort to write this book from the beginning. The workspaces at the Pittsfield Branch of the Ann Arbor District Library played a key role in helping me get the writing done in a space conducive to thinking and writing.

I've had tons and tons of help and inspiration in legaltech and innovation in law for many years. I'm sure I'll leave people off this list, but, rest assured, I'll feel guilty if I did leave you off. Thanks especially to Tom Mighell, Bill Hobson, Bert Stern, Matt Homann, Sherri Mason, JoAnna Forshee, the students in my Michigan State University College of Law classes in the 2018-2019 academic, John Tredennick, John Alber, Amanda Gioia, Dan Linna, Dan Katz, David Cowen, Cash Butler, Michael Grazio, Chip Fendell, Christie Guimond, Cat Moon, Michelle Rick, Carla Reyes, Gwynne Monahan, Whitney Johnson, Adam Camras, Mike Cappucci, Maya Markovich, Steve Gibson,

Andy Whitehead, Julie Broyles, Cat Moon, Bob Wiss, Greg Krehel, Adam Camras, Felix Marx, Kristen Sonday, Debbie Foster, Michael Kraft, Adriana Linares, Wendy Werner, Marc Lauritsen, Ron Staudt, Kevin O'Keefe, Jim Calloway, Debra Baker, Chrissie Lightfoot, Patrick McKenna, Sanjay Khanna, and many, many more.

A special thank you to Najdan Mancic for creating the cover for this book and the interior page design and production and to Grace Kennedy for proofreading and editing help. All remaining typos and mistakes are, of course, my own.

Kennedy Idea Propulsion Laboratory

The Kennedy idea Propulsion Laboratory (www.denniskennedy.com/kennedy-idea-propulsion-laboratory) is a division of Dennis Kennedy Advisory Services LLC. KIPL is the home for Dennis Kennedy's R & D efforts, custom consulting, writing, advisory board work, and innovation projects.

KIPL has created the *Legal Innovation as a Service* product for innovation leaders who want to jumpstart and course-correct their innovation projects with targeted, pre-scoped, flat fee engagements.

On KIPL's current roadmap are:

1. Panel convergence assistance packages
2. LegalTech Vendor Insights packages
3. TechPrompts—a product for getting in-house counsel up-to-speed on important technologies
4. Innovation portfolio management tools
5. Online courses

To learn more about KIPL, KIPL products and services, partnering, and custom consulting services, contact Dennis Kennedy at 734-926-5197 or dmk@denniskennedy.com.

Legal Innovation as a Service

Legal Innovation as a Service™ ("LIaaS") is a fresh approach to provide innovation leaders in legal organizations with Just-in-time, Just-enough™ guidance at key inflection points in the innovation process. LIaaS consists of pre-scoped, limited, flat fee service offerings to help you get desired feedback or help, move your effort forward, and let you get back to doing what you do best. You select the option you need from the catalog, we work together on that project, and you get quickly back on the road to success and achieving your vision.

- ► Jumpstart idea and innovation processes
- ► Avoid missteps that will cost time and money
- ► Accelerate and make smarter project selections
- ► Reality-test projects and get a market-wise second set of eyes on your efforts
- ► Get objective evaluation of investment decisions and needed course corrections

To learn more about LIaaS and other custom consulting services, contact Dennis Kennedy at 734-926-5197 or dmk@denniskennedy.com.

Speaking

Would you like me to speak at your event or create a workshop for your group? For more information, go to https://www.denniskennedy.com/dkspeaking/.

Dennis would be happy to be connected with you on LinkedIn.
See Dennis Kennedy's LinkedIn Profile by scanning this QR code.

Printed in Great
Britain
by Amazon